ENCOURAGING

PRAYERS

for

EVERY NEED

ENCOURAGING PRAYERS

for

EVERY NEED

❖━━━━━❖━❖━━━━━❖

500 Prayers for Every Season of Life

BARBOUR BOOKS
An Imprint of Barbour Publishing, Inc.

© 2017 by Barbour Publishing, Inc.

Writing and compilation by Rebecca Currington, Susan Duke, and Elece Hollis in association with Snapdragon Editorial Group™, Tulsa, Ok.

Print ISBN 978-1-68322-299-6

Published by Barbour Books, an imprint of Barbour Publishing, Inc., P.O. Box 719, Uhrichsville, Ohio 44683, www.barbourbooks.com.

Our mission is to publish and distribute inspirational products offering exceptional value and biblical encouragement to the masses.

Member of the
Evangelical Christian
Publishers Association

Printed in the United States of America.

CONTENTS

INTRODUCTION

*The earnest prayer of a righteous person has great power
and produces wonderful results.*
JAMES 5:16 NLT

Theologians have been discussing the complexities of
prayer for hundreds of years. The simplest definition,
however, may well be the best. Prayer is conversation
with God. These conversations most often take on these
familiar forms:

Prayers of Adoration exalt God's greatness and
   acknowledge our need for Him.
Prayers of Petition enumerate our perceived needs
   and ask for divine relief.
Prayers of Intercession enumerate the needs of
   others and ask for divine relief.
Prayers of Thanksgiving express thanks and
   appreciation for all God does, has done,
   and will do for us.
Prayers of Praise acknowledge God for what and
   who He is.

The prayers included in this book may fit into one or
more of these categories. We've asked our writers to
abandon their preconceived ideas of spirituality and
pull these prayers straight from their own hearts and
experiences. You may find that you relate perfectly to
many of them and easily make them your own. Others
may introduce you to a new aspect of your relationship
with God that allows you to explore His person and

character in greater depth. We pray that all these prayers will inspire you to come before your God with boldness and a greater degree of love, commitment, and understanding.

The Authors

ACCEPTANCE

*It was through reading the Scripture that I came to realize
that I could never find God's favor by trying—and failing—
to obey the laws. I came to realize that acceptance with
God comes by believing in Christ.*
GALATIANS 2:19 TLB

Heavenly Father, I have questions I realize there will
never be answers to on this side of heaven. I struggle to
understand why You've allowed the detours in my life
that have caused such pain. I realize Your peace is what
I need to accept in this season of change. Thank You for
walking with me as I seek Your presence and Your peace.
Amen.

Hello Lord, I'm so glad to be Your child today. Thanks
for accepting me just as I am. Amen.

Father, examine my heart, change me, mold me. I want
to be more accepting of the people whose paths I cross
each day. It's hard to see my own prejudices. Supposedly,
I have none, but I know better. There are those I avoid
because of the color of their skin, the way they dress,
their hairstyle. Coach me, Father, as I learn to better
accept differences. Amen.

Dear Father, thank You for accepting me as Your child,
one of the most intimate of relationships. It gives me the
courage to accept others. Amen.

ACHIEVEMENT

A desire accomplished is sweet to the soul.
PROVERBS 13:19 NKJV

Precious Lord, I'm convinced that with You, all things are possible. No goal is too great. No obstacle can keep me from my destiny. I can do nothing truly meaningful without You, but I believe I can achieve anything with Your help. Thank You for the abilities You've given to help me advance where You are leading. Amen.

Lord Jesus, bless my hands and help me achieve with them what You have planned for me. Give my actions purpose every day. Cheer me on when things seem too difficult or I struggle to reach my goals. Please pick me up when I stumble and fall. Guide me in the right direction. I know I will be able to achieve much with Your help. Amen.

Good morning, Father God. Thank You for helping me do my best today. Amen.

Father God, I pray the day will soon come when Your will for the world will be accomplished, when Your plan will be achieved, and Your Son will rule and reign over all the world. Amen.

ADDICTION/DRUG ABUSE

*Stand fast therefore in the liberty by which Christ has made us free,
and do not be entangled again with a yoke of bondage.*

GALATIANS 5:1 NKJV

Dear God, how did I end up here? Why is it so hard to stop the very thing I hate; the thing I know grieves Your heart? My soul is crying out to you, God. I can't outrun this, outwit it, or simply change my thinking. I can't fight this addiction without Your help. Draw me closer to You. I need Your overcoming power to set me free. Amen.

Dear God, please hear me as I call for help. I have succumbed to addictions that are taking over. Some have already wreaked havoc in my life and the lives of those I love. I am too weak to fight—too hurt to cry—too lost to find my way alone. I need Your help, Your strength, Your mercy. Amen.

Dear Lord, I see it all around me—a sea of souls who have surrendered their lives to alcohol, drugs, and countless other spiritual tyrants. Show me how to join in the fight to gain their freedom. Amen.

Sweet Lord, I'm so thankful for Your power to break my bonds and set me free. Amen.

*They shall stop polluting themselves with idols and their
other sins, for I will save them from all this foulness.*

EZEKIEL 37:23 TLB

Dear Lord, someone I love has become entangled in drug use. Open his eyes, Lord. Open his heart to receive the help he needs to break free from this entrapment. His life is a gift, but he's in danger of losing that gift without Your intervention. Show him that You can and will love him through his decision to call upon and depend on You. Amen.

Lord, I promise to work hard. Thank You for using my effort to help me regain my freedom. Amen.

Father, thank You for the help You have provided for me. The meetings are sometimes difficult but they are helping me believe I can change and have a better life. Guide me as I seek Your truth. Give me wisdom through the counselors and fellow participants in my program. Help me find new strength in You. Amen.

Lord God, I feel the responsibility so heavily at times. So many lives depend on me for guidance, comfort, discipline, wisdom, courage, and acceptance. I need patience to deal with the ups and downs of the former users under my care. Thank You for guiding me as I guide them to a better life. Amen.

ADOPTION

*God was kind and decided that Christ would
choose us to be God's own adopted children.*
EPHESIANS 1:5 CEV

Dear Lord, what an awesome opportunity and
responsibility You've placed before us. To know that a
little life can be changed forever because we chose to
adopt is nothing short of miraculous. Allowing us to love,
parent, and make a difference in this child's life is a great
gift. Guide us as we raise and teach this precious one to
know You. Thank You for choosing us for this amazing
assignment. Amen.

Father, how wonderful it is that you allow us to call
ourselves Your children! You adopted us into Your family
and let us call You "Abba Father," our "Daddy." Guide us
as we strive to be found worthy. Amen.

Dear God, across the world there are so many who are
without the love of a mother and father, so many who
have lost everything to war, famine, and disease. Raise
up those who will tell them of Your love and bring them
into Your family. Amen.

Oh Father, thank You so much for the precious gift of
children. Amen.

ADULTERY

Let marriage be held in honor among all,
and let the marriage bed be undefiled.
HEBREWS 13:4 ESV

Gracious Lord, I don't know how You will change the hearts of those entrapped in this situation, but I'm asking You to bring conviction and awareness of all that is at stake. Your divine intervention is critical if hearts and lives are to be healed. I'm asking You, Healer and Restorer, to bring resolution and reconciliation to these lives. You are the Potter who can remake us when we are broken. Amen.

Lord God, unfaithfulness causes such great hurt, breaking hearts and splitting families apart! It has touched each of our lives—like an epidemic; it is all around us. Save us from the intrusion of adultery, even in the hidden places of our hearts and thoughts. Set our families and communities free from its lies. Amen.

Heavenly Father, infidelity and divorce are rampant in our society. Even worse, we seem to think little about it. Help us take a stand against this evil, with love rather than condemnation. Amen.

O Lord, Your forgiveness means everything to me. Help me put away my failures and live for You. Amen.

ADVERSITY

Dear Jesus, the adversity in my life has seemed so unfair. Much of it has broken me to the point of feeling I may never recover. But through the valleys, I've come to know You in the fellowship of suffering. I've experienced the power of Your resurrection. Thank You for being my gentle Shepherd, who teaches me that nothing I go through is ever wasted, not even my tears. Amen.

Good Father, how I have struggled with troubles and trials that seem to press on every side. I know they will make me stronger, but sometimes I fear they will kill me. I fight and try to keep up a cheerful front—to keep my faith. God, help me. Even so, I don't ask that You take adversity away; only give me strength to overcome. Amen.

Father, I feel like I'm falling. Please catch me. Amen.

Dear Lord, it is in difficult times that I feel Your presence rise up strong and powerful within me. Thank You for seeing me through the trials life brings my way. Amen.

AFFLICTION

Many are the afflictions of the righteous,
but the LORD delivers him out of them all.
PSALM 34:19 NKJV

Dear God, this affliction takes me to the edge of unknown tomorrows and raises the flags of doubt and depression and weariness. It's easy to have faith when our bodies and minds are whole. But when we can't help ourselves, and answers don't come, we fight a different kind of battle. Help me give this battle to You, and remember that Your strength is perfected in my weakness. Amen.

Father, thank You for being there when I come calling. Thank You for caring about my suffering. Amen.

God, sometimes it seems like no one cares, not even You. Then I feel Your presence and realize that You do care about every ache and pain, every emotional hurt and mental wound. When I am afflicted, I will look to You. Thank You for always being there to comfort and heal. Amen.

Father God, show me how to reach out to the afflicted around me. Let my hands be Your hands of healing and comfort. Let my words deliver a sense of Your love and care. You also were afflicted. You also felt the intense pain of betrayal. Help those who find themselves in the midst of affliction. Amen.

AGING

"To your old age and gray hairs I am he, I am he who will sustain you. I have made you and I will carry you; I will sustain you and I will rescue you."
ISAIAH 46:4 NIV

Dear Lord, as I have aged, so have my parents, and now at a time when I feel myself aging, they need more help than ever from me. Give me strength beyond my years and allow me to reach out to them with patience and love. Help me remember that I'm not doing this alone. You are with me, providing the energy and wisdom I need to be a joyous helper to these people I love so dearly. Amen.

Lord, I do feel old today. I am aging so steadily and can't do half the things I used to be able to do. I find myself with time but no strength or energy. Help me settle into this new season of life. Help me stay vigilant about my heath so that I can enjoy all the years You've given me. Amen.

Father, I look to the day when time will be no more, and we will be free of these aging and imperfect bodies. Thank You for my life and the days You have given me here on earth. Help me use them well. Amen.

Sweet Lord, the longer I live, the more I love You and acknowledge my need for You. Amen.

ALCOHOL

Don't get drunk with wine, which leads
to reckless actions, but be filled by the Spirit.
EPHESIANS 5:18 HCSB

Lord, save me from myself. I am nothing without Your
help. Amen.

Heavenly Father, so many need to be rescued from the
bondage of alcohol. They pretend to be in control while
the truth is that they are being controlled. I know that
every person is precious in Your sight. Help each one
see that alcohol will never heal their hurts or give them
peace. Clear their minds to recognize the hope that is
much greater than an instant need to dull their senses.
Shine Your light, Lord. Show them how to love and
value themselves just as You do. Amen.

Father, I know so many who have succumbed to alcohol
abuse. This tragedy has wrecked lives and destroyed
families. A child once asked me why You made alcohol. I
wasn't sure what answer would be appropriate. Show me
how to provide mercy and kindness to those who are in
alcohol's clutches and wisdom and counsel to those who
have not yet encountered its dangers. Amen.

Father God, alcohol, like so many other things in this
world, can be used for both good and evil. Help us as we
navigate the dangers around us. Amen.

AMBITION

Where envy and selfish ambition exist,
there is disorder and every kind of evil.
JAMES 3:16 HCSB

Gracious Father, while I want to be diligent and passionate, and have the confidence that my goals are attainable, I never want ambition itself to become my priority. Teach me to discern the trappings of unbalanced ambitions. Help me always remember that my true significance will always be found in You. Thank You for giving me what is needed to reach my goals and fulfill Your highest calling for my life. Amen.

O God, I know You want me to succeed in life, but keep a rein on my ambition and drive. Help me stay aware of my family, coworkers, and friends so that I can follow my dream without neglecting or harming anyone else. Keep me moving forward with a godly heart and mind so that what I aim for will be something that glorifies You and blesses others. Amen.

Holy Father, thank You for placing within my heart a desire to succeed. Help me make the most of every opportunity while refusing to allow my ambition to make me selfish and self-centered. May my greatest ambition be to know and love You better. Amen.

Father, all I want for my life is to love You more and be more like You. Amen.

ANNIVERSARY

"Put Me in remembrance."
ISAIAH 43:26 NKJV

Dear Lord, anniversaries have a way of bringing back so many memories. When it's a painful memory, as it is for me today, the tears flow, and my heart hurts. Lord, be with me and help me remember the blessings of love, knowing my tears are the evidence of the gift given. Amen.

Father, thank You for the person You gave me to spend my life with! As a matchmaker, You're the best. We invite You to join with us as we celebrate this special day. Amen.

Lord, it is almost here again and I am not ready. Some anniversaries are happy, but this one hurts. It is a day I don't want to remember but am never able to forget. It is a day when a dream ended. Help my heart heal, Father. Give me strength through this hard day coming and help me move on. Amen.

Lord God, there are so many anniversaries in my life, but none as sweet as the anniversary of the day I asked You to come into my life. Thank You for all the blessings and privileges You've poured out on me through the years. Amen.

ANGER

Using good sense can put out the flames of anger.
PROVERBS 29:8 CEV

Dear Jesus, I know my anger isn't pleasing to You. And I know I must forgive and let go of all offenses in order to be free. I don't want bitterness to take root in my heart. Choosing to forgive is my hope and the key that unlocks the prison in which I've placed myself. Show me Your unfolding purpose as I confess my anger and invite Your love to fill me and flow through me again. Amen.

Dear Jesus, the Bible says You got angry, yet You never sinned. You were angry with people who were religious and yet cheated their fellow man. My anger is me centered—someone did not do what suited *me*, someone slighted *me*, someone hurt *me*. Clearly I need to get over myself and exchange my anger for love and forgiveness. Amen.

Father God, I praise You for turning Your anger away and forgiving my sins and failures. May I please You by surrendering the anger I've directed at those who have wronged me. Amen.

Lord, help me be angry about the things that make You angry. Amen.

ANXIETY

"Do not be anxious about your life, what you will eat or what
you will drink, nor about your body, what you will put on.
Is not life more than food, and the body more than clothing?"
MATTHEW 6:25 ESV

Heavenly Father, giving You my worries and letting go of
stress is easier said than done. As I take this step of faith
and ask You to calm my anxious heart, help me take a
deep breath and fully release every fear and worry to You.
Be my resting place, Father, and help me remember that
You are so much more than enough. Amen.

God, this is such a problem for me. I know, troubles
are part of this life and they will come. Please, guard
my mind from needless anxiety. I'm thankful for Your
promise never to leave me; that, like a good daddy,
You are always holding my hand. You tell me not to be
anxious and fearful. Help me grow out of my worries and
into Your peace. Amen.

Father, I just want to wrap myself up in You today. Please
help me feel better. Amen.

Lord God, all around me the winds of anxiety are
blowing. Thank You for the peace You've given me from
the inside out. Show me how to share that peace—Your
peace—with those who are anxious. Amen.

ASSURANCE

Let us draw near with a sincere heart in full assurance of faith,
having our hearts sprinkled clean from an evil conscience
and our bodies washed with pure water.
HEBREWS 10:22 NASB

Dear Jesus, give me a strong faith. The kind of childlike faith that believes in quiet wonder that You know my needs and hear my prayers. When answers don't come, and mountains don't move, impress on my heart the assurance that You are working behind the scenes on my behalf in ways I can't comprehend. Amen.

Heavenly Father, please help me feel Your presence. I need to know You're near. Amen.

Father of All, thank You for the times when I am able to rest in the assurance that You love me and will always be here to care for me. Things change so quickly these days but You are always the same. I count on that in the midst of every crisis. Your love is unconditional; Your kindness is constant; Your justice is perfect; Your holiness is unerring. I know I can always call on You. Amen.

Heavenly Father, some say we can't be sure of heaven or even life after death, but Your Word is full of assurances that I need not fear anything because You will always be with me in this life and whatever comes after. Amen.

ATTITUDE

*May the God who gives endurance and
encouragement give you the same attitude of
mind toward each other that Christ Jesus had.*
ROMANS 15:5 NIV

Father, thank You for being my "attitude changer." Amen.

Precious Lord, the attitude of my heart means so much.
It's always when I speak or act out of emotion that I find
myself in trouble. Help me think and pray first, Lord.
Temper my emotions with Your grace and love, and help
me adapt every attitude of my heart and mind to a place
where they are pleasing to You. Amen.

Lord, my attitude has improved lately. Thanks for
helping me get stronger and overcome the negativity that
has plagued me for so many years. Attitude is such a life
changer. I want to be healthy in mind and spirit and to
be a cheerful, happy person who is capable of bringing
joy to the lives of others. Keep working with me, Lord.
Amen.

Lord, I want my attitude to reflect Yours in that when
You were wronged, You forgave; when You were
wounded, You continued to love. I want to be just like
You, my Father. Amen.

BANKRUPTCY

Steep your life in God-reality, God-initiative,
God-provisions. Don't worry about missing out.
You'll find all your everyday human concerns will be met.
MATTHEW 6:33 MSG

Gracious Father, only You know how this financial
burden will be resolved. As I surrender each detail
to You, help me learn and grow and become more
responsible from this experience. You are my source
and my provider. Help me be a good steward of Your
provisions and Your help. Amen.

Dear God, I have failed with money. Finances are a weak
area in my life. Help me learn and grow through this crisis.
Chasten me when I start to feel sorry for myself, and
remind me to use that energy to work hard to overcome
what has been lost. Be merciful to me and help me learn
discipline. Guide me and teach me so that I can pay my
bills and support my family well in the future. Amen.

Thank You, Father. I may not have money and
possessions, but I will always have You. Amen.

Dear Father, thank You for reminding me that while I
may be financially bankrupt, I am not bankrupt morally,
emotionally, or spiritually. Of all those, money trouble
is the least important and the easiest to overcome. It
certainly doesn't feel good, but I know You will be by my
side as always, smoothing out the path ahead. Amen.

BETRAYAL

It is not a foe who rises up against me—otherwise I could hide from him. But it is you, a man who is my peer, my companion and good friend!
PSALM 55:12–13 HCSB

Dear God, I never saw this emotional storm coming. Like a tornado that hits with great destructive power, my world has been shattered. The only place I know to run is to You, God. As I give You my broken heart, I also thank You for being my safe place, and the one who will never leave me, forsake me, or betray me. Amen.

Father, it's difficult to believe that someone I trusted so fully has betrayed me. It wouldn't hurt so much except that he was like a brother, a friend I had faith in. You, Lord, are a friend closer than a brother! Thank You for comforting me and leading me to a place of forgiveness. I don't ever want bitterness to grow in my heart. Amen.

Lord God, my friend has betrayed me and it hurts. Nevertheless, I choose to forgive just as You forgave those who betrayed You. Amen.

Father, I'm so glad that You have promised never to betray me. Amen.

BIRTHDAY

All the stages of my life were spread out before you,
the days of my life all prepared before I'd even lived one day.
PSALM 139:16 MSG

Dear Lord, thank You for the blessing of my birthday.
My life is a gift, given by You. Help me remember that
I was born with a purpose and a longing to know You.
Help me never take the moments of Your gracious gift
for granted. Amen.

Father, today is my birthday. I know it isn't very
important in the scheme of things, but it does celebrate
the beginning of my life and Your investment in me.
Thanks for creating me and making me unique. And
speaking of gifts, I hope my life is a gift to You. Amen.

Lord, don't worry. It will always be Your birthday in my
heart. Amen.

My Dear Father, I know You are ageless—You have no
beginning and no end. For that reason, celebrating Your
birthday seems a little odd. But I know You understand
our human limitations and frailties. You understand the
simple ways we mark time. So I celebrate today Your
God-life and the great wonder that is Your presence in
all my days. Amen.

BLESSINGS

Blessed be the God and Father of our Lord Jesus Christ,
who has blessed us in Christ with every spiritual
blessing in the heavenly places.
EPHESIANS 1:3 NRSV

Dear Jesus, Your blessings on my life are many. When I try to count them, my heart overflows. Even during times that didn't seem like a blessing, You showed me that Your will and plan for my life was being worked out for my ultimate good. Thank You for the blessings You have so generously given and the blessings You have yet to pour out on me. Most of all, Jesus, thank You for the blessing of knowing I belong to You. Amen.

Dear Lord Jesus, help me better show my thankfulness to You by being a blessing to others. I'm aware that I often miss opportunities because I'm too busy with my own concerns. I would ask You to show me how to make time for encouraging words, generous giving, and kind actions that truly bless others. In this way, I pray that I will also bless You. Amen.

Showers of blessings, Lord. You shower me with blessings every day. Amen.

Heavenly Father, I float in a sea of blessings. The more I appreciate them, the more I see. They are too great in number to count. My deep desire is to bless You in return by the way I live my life. Amen.

BROKEN HEART

The LORD is near to the brokenhearted,
and saves the crushed in spirit.
PSALM 34:18 NRSV

Dear Lord, my heart is broken; and right now, this brokenness feels like hopelessness. I've always believed that You are the mender of broken hearts; so I'm asking You, Lord, to help me believe my own words. As I give You the broken pieces, I trust that in time, You will make my heart whole again. Amen.

Lord, my child has a broken heart, and I know there is no way I can fix it. She has been hurt beyond iodine and bandages. Give me the skill to guide her to Your arms, because I know there she can find comfort and hope. Show me how I can help her without coddling, denial, excuses, or harmful self-pity. Thank You, Lord. Amen.

My actions have broken Your heart, Lord. Show me how to make You smile again. Amen.

Lord God, somehow I thought that having You in my life would mean I'd never hurt this badly again. Now I realize that heartache will still visit me. The difference is that I will never again suffer alone. You will be here to comfort, heal, and dry my tears. Thank You! Amen.

BURDENS

*Carry each other's burdens, and in this
way you will fulfill the law of Christ.*
GALATIANS 6:2 NIV

Dear God, every area of my life is challenging my faith
and my emotional stamina. One problem seems to
compound another. The burdens that are weighing down
my spirit are too heavy to keep carrying. Help me lay
each and every concern at Your feet once and for all,
God. As I close my eyes and place them there, help me
also leave them there and trust them to Your care. Amen.

God, this burden is too heavy for me, but I know it is not
too heavy for You. You have taught me Your truth, and I
know that Your mercy and goodness are things I can count
on. You have been there to do the heavy lifting when I
simply couldn't carry my burdens any longer. You have
never failed me—even when the burden was of my own
making. Thank You for being my burden-bearer. Amen.

This burden, Lord. This one right here! I keep picking it
up again and again. Stop me, please! Amen.

Lord Jesus, help me see my burdens as opportunities to
experience Your constant care and deliverance. Thank
You for being my burden-lifter. Amen.

CAREER

Your words are a flashlight to light the path
ahead of me and keep me from stumbling.
PSALM 119:105 TLB

Dear Lord, a new path is awaiting me that is both exciting and daunting. I believe this is part of Your plan for my life, and I thank You for this wonderful opportunity. Guide me in my decisions. Help me be diligent, responsible, and ever thankful for Your provision. Thank You for the relief it brings from financial strain and the satisfaction my career provides. Amen.

Dear God, guide me in my studies and in the many choices the next few years of my life will bring. I am not certain if I should choose the most inviting job or the one that pays the most. I just want to find the job that You have in mind for me. Give me courage to follow Your plan wherever it leads me. Amen.

People keep asking me what I plan to do with my life, Lord. The answer is, *"I have no idea!"* Could You help me sort it out? Amen.

Lord God, thank You for the opportunities You've given me to use my talents and skills. Show me how to avoid the politics and resentments that come with the workplace so that I can reach my full potential while helping my coworkers reach theirs. Amen.

CARES

When the cares of my heart are many,
your consolations cheer my soul.
Psalm 94:19 ESV

Dear Father, I'm reminded in Your Word that You will perfect everything that concerns me. That's a big and merciful promise, Father. It's a promise that causes me to pause, breathe deeply, and release the heaviness of my cares to You. Loving Father, thank You for caring for me so tenderly and completely. Amen.

Dear Lord, I have cares knocking at every door of my life right now, and I don't want to answer any of them. I want to trust in You and let those cares go on down the road or, better yet, languish and die out on the road— never finding a welcome from me. I want to rest in Your peace—the peace that is so miraculous, it cannot be understood. Amen.

Father God, show me how to be cognizant of the cares others are carrying, so that I may offer my support, prayers, and encouragement. It's easy to get caught up in my own affairs and fail to notice the hurting people around me. Amen.

Lord, I keep taking on other people's problems. Instead of helping them, it just weighs me down. Remind me to encourage others to release their cares to You. Amen.

CHALLENGES

Consider it a sheer gift, friends, when tests and challenges
come at you from all sides. You know that under pressure,
your faith-life is forced into the open and shows its true colors.
JAMES 1:2–3 MSG

Dear Lord, sometimes the challenges of life cause
me to feel like I'm living from one emergency to the
next. I know it's not Your will for me to be exhausted,
emotionally frazzled, or defeated. Help me face my
challenges by looking in the only place real answers are
found—Your Word. I'm standing firm in the belief that
in seeking You, I will find You; my advocate, my comfort,
and my constant hope. Amen.

Challenge me, Lord, to become everything *You* think I
can be. Amen.

Father, how You must shake Your head at us in
amazement. We love competition. We love games,
contests, and puzzles. We climb mountains and cross seas
just to see if we can. Yet when we face true challenges,
like a difficult decision, an unexpected illness, a painful
injury, or a crumbling marriage, we quit. At least, I
know I do. Please give me the guts to fight through the
challenges in my life. Amen.

Dear Lord, I'm not sure why You've placed such a challenging person in my life. Maybe it was to test me or refine
me or simply to take my eyes off myself. Help me honor
You each day as I strive to respond with love. Amen.

CHANGE

*[God] is looking for those with changed hearts and minds. Whoever
has that kind of change in his life will get his praise from God.*
ROMANS 2:29 TLB

Dear God, while I realize that change is inevitable in
my life, I am struggling with giving up what is familiar
and comfortable. Help me remember as changes come
that You are the God who never changes. Steady my
heart and help me trust You to take me safely into the
unknown. Amen.

Father God, I struggle with change and complain about
my present. How hard I must be to work with! Help me
face changes when they come—embrace them even as
beautiful new steps in my journey. Give me courage and
creativity to see the changes as gifts. Teach me to face
new places, new circumstances, and new paths with heart
and humor. Amen.

Father God, I recognize that change is almost always a
good thing in my life—and yet, I balk every single time.
Help me look change squarely in the eye and move
forward out of my love and respect for You. Amen.

Here I am, Lord. Change me! Amen.

CHILDREN/GRANDCHILDREN

*Jesus said, "Leave the children alone, and don't try to
keep them from coming to Me, because the kingdom
of heaven is made up of people like this."*
MATTHEW 19:14 HCSB

Dear Father, as much as I desire to be a good parent to
my children, give me insight and awareness to also learn
from them. Thank You for the opportunity and blessing of
influencing such precious hearts and lives. Help me always
convey that their lives are a gift to me from You. Amen.

Lord, I thank You for the children in my life. Though
I may not have little ones around my feet, I do have
youngsters to love and encourage, be they grandchildren,
neighborhood kids, relatives, or church children. If there
are none in my path, help me find some to help, guide,
and love through writing letters, teaching, volunteering,
coaching, or using any other way You please. Let me say as
You did, "Let the little children come unto me." Amen.

Father God, thank You for showing me how to be a good
parent to the children You've given me. You've shown me
by modeling what a lovingly parent should be—strong and
tender, consistent and merciful, holy and forgiving. Amen.

Such charming playmates, Lord. Use them to teach me
to play again. Amen.

*But from everlasting to everlasting the LORD's love is with those
who fear him, and his righteousness with their children's children.*
PSALM 103:17 NIV

Dear God, thank You for my grandchildren. I could have never imagined what a joyful blessing they would be in my life. Through them, You've given me more love, more moments of celebration, and more gratitude than I could have thought possible. Help me be the kind of grandparent they need and can always look up to. As I love them, help me also demonstrate and impart Your love to them. Amen.

Father, there are times when I find grandparenting exhausting! My nerves are older now and my patience wears thin. And yet even now I long to see them again. What a blessing it is to have these precious creatures to call my own. They are endearing and captivating. Help me deal with my grandkids needs and wants without spoiling them, while showing love, patience, and forbearance. Amen.

Dear Father, thank You for blessing me with my first grandchild. I had no idea I would feel so connected, so in love. I just look at this little one and my eyes fill with tears of happiness. Help me be a wise grandparent. Amen.

CHOICES/DECISIONS

"You did not choose Me but I chose you, and appointed you that you would go and bear fruit, and that your fruit would remain."
JOHN 15:16 NASB

Dear Lord, thank You for the free will You've given me to make my own choices. Help me seek Your counsel and wisdom before using that freedom. As I desire to choose what is Your best for me, I pray that each choice I make will ultimately glorify You. Amen.

Father, I face choices daily. Simple ones like what to wear or which tea to sip have little if any bearing on life. But some are life-changing. Help me follow You in all the choices I face—the big and the small. Forgive me when I push ahead and make choices that draw me away from You. And thank You for helping me make choices that are good for me and all those around me. Amen.

I choose You, Lord, today, tomorrow, and every day! Amen.

Lord God, before I ever knew You, You chose me to be Yours. I may never understand why You would want me, but I accept Your choice with gratitude and love in my heart. Thank You for calling me Your child and allowing me to call You my father. Amen.

Choose this day whom you will serve.
JOSHUA 24:15 NRSV

Dear Lord, it's so easy to make hasty and unwise decisions. When I've done so in the past, I've realized they often became regrets in my life. Clear my mind so I can better think through all the considerations. Help me, without stress and haste, take the time needed to still my mind and spirit as I seek Your wisdom and Your will in this matter. Amen.

Lord, my brain is a swirl of questions: Should I do this or go there? Should I buy this? Should I say this or keep my comments to myself? Some days I feel lost in the giant swirling universe. I ask for Your guidance as I find my way forward. Help me listen carefully to the wise people You have placed in my life, and show me the purest truth as I spend time in Your Word. Amen.

Help me decide each day to follow You, Lord. Amen.

Father God, thank You for providing Your wisdom and understanding through the years. I see the fruit of that in my life today. So much of life is lived in the dark, but walking with You dispels the darkness and lights the way. I will always need Your wisdom and guidance. Thank You for always giving it so freely. Amen.

CHRONIC ILLNESS/SICKNESS

While the sun was setting, all those who had any who were
sick with various diseases brought them to Him; and laying
His hands on each one of them, He was healing them.
LUKE 4:40 NASB

Heavenly Father, my friend is suffering. I don't know how to help her physically, but I'm asking for merciful relief and healing from the pain she's enduring. Help me be sensitive to her needs, and guide me as I seek to be a comforting friend who will bring encouragement in her greatest time of need. Amen.

Dear Lord, it's hard to watch someone I love suffering. Sometimes I wonder why You allow it. Even though I don't understand, I trust You. I know that You love us and You are with us, helping us bear whatever pain we must go through. Show me how to bring comfort with my words and deeds. Amen.

I don't know what tomorrow will bring, Lord, but my hope is in You. Amen.

Holy Father, my body aches, and I must admit that sometimes I feel like giving up, like I can't fight this any longer. Instead, I choose to trust You and seek Your comfort. I know You are a God who heals. I pray that You would touch my body and make me whole. Relieve my suffering. Give me reason to go on. Amen.

Their prayer, if offered in faith, will heal him,
for the Lord will make him well.
JAMES 5:15 TLB

Heavenly Father, when You died on the cross for my sins, You also died for my healing. Strengthen me and strengthen my belief that the sickness I'm battling has already been paid for and covered by You. Let faith rise up in me as I trust You with all the days of my life. Amen.

Thank You, Lord God, that sickness has no power over You. Amen.

Father, it seems like when I'm sick, all my problems appear insurmountable. I see mountains everywhere I look. I need to get my eyes adjusted. Allow me to exchange my eyes of fear for eyes of faith. Help me get my body and soul back under Your control. Amen.

Father, while I'm waiting for Your healing hand, I cherish the opportunity to spend time in Your presence. I'm afraid and weary and hurting. It's a relief to feel You close and know You care. I pray that when this is over, I will be stronger, wiser. I pray I will also be more empathetic with others who are going through times of illness. Amen.

CHURCH DISCORD/
CHURCH FAMILY

Above all, put on love—the perfect bond of unity.
COLOSSIANS 3:14 HCSB

Dear God, it must hurt Your heart when you see Your children warring against each other. I'm asking You to speak to hearts in such a way that will cause them to set aside their differences for the good of Your Kingdom. Bring unity of Spirit and purpose to Your church, God. Let my part be as a prayer covering to petition for Your healing grace and restoration. Amen.

Lord, help us find our way out of this mess. We are Your people and yet we struggle to get along. We are like a bunch of sheep—silly disobedient sheep who all want to go a different way. Some of us follow one path—some another. Come to us, Lord. Forgive us. Heal us and help us resolve our differences with love and respect for one another and for You. Amen.

Let peace and unity begin with me, Lord. Amen.

Father, You made Your will clear when You prayed for unity. I ask for that as well. I know that's possible only when You change our hearts. I offer mine. Expose any selfishness, pride, lack of love—anything that prevents me from coming together in unity with my sisters and brothers. Amen.

Show family affection to one another with brotherly love.
ROMANS 12:10 HCSB

Father, those of us You call Your own are really a big family. Help us find friendship, form brotherly bonds, and learn to be sensitive to one another's needs. May we learn to trust and pray for each other. Help each of us put others first. Thank You for the gift of spiritual family. Amen.

Gracious Father, much like my biological family, my church family consists of many different personalities. Sometimes, there are conflicting ideas and disagreements. The fellowship of my church family is a vital part of my life and walk with You. Help me love and serve through the difficult times, making it a priority to love unconditionally as You love me. Amen.

What a joy to be part of the family of God, Lord! Amen.

Heavenly Father, it is because You are our spiritual Father that we can see ourselves as spiritual brothers and sisters. Thank for the joy and comfort that brings to all our lives. It is even more appreciated when we are separated from our earthly families by miles or issues. Amen.

CIRCUMSTANCES

*I am sending him to you for this very purpose, that he
may know your circumstances and comfort your hearts.*
COLOSSIANS 4:8 NKJV

Precious Lord, help me surrender the circumstances of
my life to Your tender care. Help me stay laser focused on
You, unshaken by what I see, hear, or feel. Help me press
on beyond what looks impossible. I trust and rely on Your
strength for my safety and see You as the source for all of
my needs. Thank You for steadying my steps as You lead
me to a higher ground of faith. Amen.

God, I have to be honest—after all, You know my
thoughts. Sometimes I feel like You are far away and my
circumstances are too small to matter to You. At those
times, I feel frustrated and afraid. In the Bible, You invite
us to put our circumstances in Your hands and allow You
to prove Your faithfulness. Thank You for hearing my
prayer. Amen.

Lord God, when I stop to think, I realize that my
positive circumstances always outweigh my negative
circumstances. Your blessings always dominate my life.
Help me keep my eyes on that rather than focusing on
those things that are not going as expected. I believe You
are a good God who loves me. Amen.

The circumstances of my life, Lord, are all in Your
hands. Amen.

COMFORT

Blessed be the God and Father of our Lord Jesus Christ, the Father of mercies and God of all comfort, who comforts us in all our tribulation, that we may be able to comfort those who are in any trouble, with the comfort with which we ourselves are comforted by God.

2 Corinthians 1:3–4 NKJV

Gracious Father, help me seek and rely on the true comfort of Your Holy Spirit, remembering that You have provided all I need when my heart is overwhelmed. Help me run only to You when I need consolation and the kind of compassion that You offer me, Your child. Amen.

Lord, when I need comfort, You are always there waiting to help. How sad that some days I call on You only if I am scared or lonely, panicked or in crisis. I can say though that whenever I call on You, You always hear me and answer. You've always sent me help. Thank You, Lord, for the comfort You are to me, even when I fail to appreciate Your love. Amen.

Help me, Lord, to be a warm, soft, comforting presence for those who need me. Amen.

Holy Father, when I need comfort, I always run to You. Friends sometimes fail me. Family often fails to notice my pain, but You are always there, ready and able to take me in Your arms. I like, too, that You don't coddle me. Instead You urge me to stand up and give thanks for the good things in my life. Thank You for being such a good Father. Amen.

COMMITMENT

*Commit your way to the LORD; trust in Him,
and He will act, making your righteousness
shine like the dawn, your justice like the noonday.*
PSALM 37:5–6 HCSB

Dear God, commitment can be a little frightening. I often struggle with believing I can stay the course and fulfill my obligations, knowing life has a way of throwing roadblocks in my way. Help me trust that You will always make a way when my heart is steadfast in my goal to live in the center of Your will. Amen.

Father God, I remember well the day I gave my life to You. I've kept my commitment, but I'm aware that I've been able to do that only because You've kept Your commitment to me. When I waver, You stand strong. When I fail, You forgive. When I become distracted, You draw me back to You. I am amazed by the depth of Your love for me. It makes me want to give myself to You again and again. Amen.

Lord, You know I have trouble staying focused. Keep me focused on You. Amen.

Sweet Father, thank You for remaining committed to Your plan of salvation. All of us are so imperfect. Not a one is without sin. And yet, You have continued to hold out Your hand to us—to me. You have continued to love, forgive, and keep Your promises. Thank You. Amen.

COMMUNITY

Take your stand with God's loyal community and live.
PROVERBS 11:19 MSG

Dear Jesus, I know You've designed our lives with a calling and desire to be part of something greater than ourselves. Help me be a contributing part of Your vision for my community. Thank You for the blessing of sharing life and purpose with others. I'm grateful for the opportunity to partner with others to make a difference in the lives of those around me. Amen.

Lord Jesus, I live in a rural area, but over time, I've come to know the neighboring farmers and ranchers, the preachers of rural churches nearby, the school bus drivers, and postal workers. How do I fit in? What is my part in this picture? Do my neighbors know that I pray, that I will help in trouble and sickness and need? Help me love my community as You loved those in Your daily life on earth. Help me be more like You. Amen.

I long to be part of a community, Lord. Show me where I belong. Amen.

Dear Father, I pray for my community, this place that has become part of me as I have become part of it. Help me do all I can to stand up for those who have no voice and reach out to those who have needs. Thank You for planting me in this place. Amen.

CONFESSION

My sacrifice is a humble spirit, O God;
you will not reject a humble and repentant heart.
PSALM 51:17 GNT

Merciful Lord, as I share with You the deepest secrets of my heart, I ask You to forgive me and help me forgive myself. I want to be real and invite You into the broken places that I've created. I confess my carelessness and ask You to heal me and hold me in Your hands where I find grace and become aware of Your tender mercies. Amen.

Lord God, it is easy to point out the failings of others, but much harder to reveal my own. Still I know I can hide nothing from You. You see all. You are also forgiving. My sins break my heart, and I know they break Yours. Thank You for pointing me toward Your perfect holiness and Your generous grace. Amen.

Father in Heaven, I have failed You—again. Part of me wants to hold back, pull away, ashamed to face You, but there is no forgiveness until I reach out for it. Thank You for Your faithful love that gives me the courage I need to approach You, knowing that I will walk away clean and forgiven. Amen.

I'm ready, Lord, to confess before heaven and earth that You are my God! Amen.

CONFIDENCE

Reverence for the LORD gives confidence and security.
PROVERBS 14:26 GNT

Dear Lord, as a vessel of flesh with limitations and vulnerabilities, help me remember that You and Your power dwells inside me. Lord, I know that in You there is no condemnation or intimidation. Let my confidence arise from being Your child, destined to be who and what You've created me to be. Amen.

I have this confidence, Lord, that You will never leave me nor forsake me. Amen.

Lord God, I've watched the Olympics, and I've seen the confidence each winner has to have to compete well. I need that kind of certainty to be the best I can be, but my confidence often fails me. Help me, Lord, to see the value in trying even if I don't "take home gold." Give me courage to step up when You need me. Amen.

Heavenly Father, that task You have set before me looks to me like a huge obstacle in my path. I ask You to give me the confidence I need—the confidence that You are guiding and directing, strengthening and inspiring me as I go forward. Amen.

CONFLICT

*Though a host encamp against me, my heart will not fear;
though war arise against me, in spite of this I shall be confident.*
PSALM 27:3 NASB

Heavenly Father, I'm in the middle of a conflict that has brought me a lot of strife and regret. I've even allowed it to stop the peaceful flow of Your Spirit in me. Help me be still enough to feel Your presence and release anything that is hindering my trust in You. I ask for wisdom and grace as I work to resolve this situation. Amen.

What do you do when someone just won't leave you alone, Lord? Things at school couldn't be worse. Show me how to cope and guide me to an adult who can protect me. Amen.

Father, I have seen plenty of conflicts, and I don't see any good in them. Forgive us. Forgive me. Place in me the heart and voice of a peacemaker. Let me be the first to repent and walk away from accusation and faultfinding. Let conflict end and peace begin with me. Amen.

Dear Lord, from my window, the world outside looks calm and peaceful. But I know I'm handicapped by my nearsightedness. Beyond what my eyes can see is a world rife with conflict, war, anger, and tragedy. We human beings just can't seem to stop hurting each other. My hope rests in knowing that You are the Prince of Peace. Have mercy on us, I pray. Amen.

CONSCIENCE

Pray for us, for we are sure that we have a good conscience,
desiring to conduct ourselves honorably in all things.
HEBREWS 13:18 NASB

Dear God, when it might have been easier to let something that was wrong slide, You quickened my spirit and my conscience to take the high road. I'm so thankful I listened, heeded, and asked for Your guidance instead of relying on my own way of thinking. Thank You for giving me a conscience that helps ensure all will be well in my soul. Amen.

Speak to me, Lord, when I do right and also when I do wrong. Amen.

Lord God, once I had a strong conscience, but these days, I've noticed my conscience has quieted down. Lord, I want to be like you—to flee sin and fight sin with the truth. Sometimes though I fail to see my shortcomings. Don't let me go numb to sin. Stir my conscience so that I can be pleasing in Your sight. Thank You. Amen.

Lord in Heaven, I know my sin separates me from You. For that reason above all others, I want a strong conscience. I want that inner voice to cry danger when sin is in the neighborhood. Thank You for this God-given awareness that protects my relationship with You. Amen.

CONTENTMENT

Serving God does make us very rich,
if we are satisfied with what we have.
1 TIMOTHY 6:6 NCV

Dear Lord, I'm asking You to replace the emptiness and frustration I feel inside with Your Spirit. You are the only One who can give me the serenity of a contented heart. Fill me afresh with Your presence, and help me walk in the harmony and fulfillment of Your perfect peace. Amen.

Lord, I know the things I possess cannot make me happy. I should be content in every circumstance and with whatever I have—finding true happiness in You. You are all I need. You are my provider and the treasure that I search for. You have given Your life to save mine, and You have forgiven me again and again. Sow contentment in my heart and let it root and sprout. Amen.

Lord God, thank You for Your goodness to me. You have given me all I have and all I need. Knowing this fills my heart with gratitude and inspires me to lift my voice in praise and thanksgiving. Amen.

I only have two friends, Lord. Some people say that's not nearly enough for someone my age. My friends are good people and are good to me. We have fun together, and I love them. Is it all right to be content with two friends? Amen.

COUNSEL

Listen to advice and accept correction,
and in the end you will be wise.
PROVERBS 19:20 NCV

Heavenly Father, some decisions I'm facing require much wisdom, discernment, and direction. I'm asking You to lead me to someone I can trust, someone I can talk to, someone who can offer me wise counsel. As I place my trust in You to help me understand and take the steps I need to take, I'm also trusting You to place someone with the gift of wisdom in my path to bring sound reasoning and counsel. Amen.

Lord, advice is easy to sweep aside. Good or bad? Counsel is deeper and usually something I asked for. Still, I find much of it hard to hear and harder to act on. Why am I so stubborn and set in my ways? I need to take good counsel. You have given me guidance, Lord. Help me act on it. Amen.

Everywhere I turn, someone is trying to tell me what to do. I don't know who to listen to. Can You help me figure it out? Amen.

Dear Lord, so often I forget to ask for Your counsel and advice. I go running off with my plan in mind. For that reason, I fail as often as I succeed. I want to be wise—the kind of wise that comes from listening to the only One who sees the future and knows the intent of the heart. You are the best counselor, and You've invited me to come to You. Thanks for Your gift of counsel. Amen.

COURAGE

Be on your guard; stand firm in the faith;
be courageous; be strong.
1 CORINTHIANS 16:13 NIV

Dear Lord, I'm facing a situation that seems to be impossible to conquer. Fear has overtaken the courage I need to fight this giant. I know, just as David faced Goliath, my trust in You must be bigger than my fear. Your Word assures me that You are not only with me in every battle that I face, but that the battle belongs to You. Help me remember that I can do all things because You are my strength and my shield. Give me the courage to lay fear aside and fight as an overcomer. Amen.

Father, the world seems to misunderstand the word *courage*. They say courage is standing for the underdog and reprimanding hypocrites. Courage is an innocent man taking punishment for the guilty party. Courage, they think, is speaking the truth and standing tall. Come to think of it, they are right. Courage is You. Amen.

Stuff goes on every day at school, Lord. I need courage to stand up for myself and others. Amen.

Lord God, it takes courage to live as a true Christian. I want to be a Christian in more than name only. I want to stand with You for what is right, speak out against what is wrong, and live in anticipation of seeing others turn to You because of my example. Most of all, I want to live in a way that will bring a smile of approval to Your face. Amen.

CRITICISM

*Whoever heeds life-giving correction
will be at home among the wise.*
PROVERBS 15:31 NIV

Dear God, as much as possible, I try to guard my heart against the temptation to be a critical person—but there are moments, I admit, when I give in to negative and judgmental thinking. This is not who I want to be. Help me have an attitude of grace, and redirect my observations of others to focus on what is good. Help me develop a more positive and merciful attitude. Amen.

Lord, my brother and sister drive me crazy, but when I tell my mom, she says I'm being critical. I think I'm just telling the truth. Can You help me learn the difference? Amen.

Father, help me deal with the criticism that seems to swirl around me somedays. More than that, help me discern what criticism will make me a better person and what will stifle me with condemnation. Remind me daily that the criticism You send my way is able to bring me closer to the person You created me to be. Amen.

Heavenly Father, I don't know why I seem so determined to find fault with others. I think it might be that judging others takes the focus off of my own flaws. I surrender to You my need to point out wrong and ask that You would make me an encourager instead. Amen.

DEATH OR ILLNESS OF A CHILD

While he spoke these things to them, behold, a ruler came
and worshiped Him, saying, "My daughter has just died,
but come and lay Your hand on her and she will live."
MATTHEW 9:18 NKJV

Dear Jesus, life wasn't supposed to turn out this way. A
parent should never have to bury a child. I have no place
to put this unspeakable grief, Jesus, but I'm running to
You and asking You to help me. Hear the words my
broken heart cannot speak. Open Your arms, and let me
find a place for my heart to rest in the comfort, hope, and
safety of Your merciful presence. Amen.

Lord, my friend has lost her son to a senseless accident
caused by a careless driver. I can only imagine what she
must be going through. I shudder when I consider the
pain she must feel every time she thinks of him, faces
an empty chair at dinner, sees his things, or even looks
around and remembers. Help her make it through the
hurt and misery. Comfort her heart. Renew her faith in
Your love and protect her from bitterness. Amen.

Father God, I would rather be sick myself than see my
child suffering like this. I ask You to bring relief to this
situation. I pray that You will reach down and touch my
child with Your healing hands. Then show me how to
stand by, waiting patiently for Your deliverance. Amen.

DEATH OR ILLNESS OF A PARENT

The LORD will strengthen him on his bed of illness;
You will sustain him on his sickbed.
PSALM 41:3 NKJV

Dear heavenly Father, my heart is breaking as I witness the pain and physical suffering my parent is going through. As I pray for relief and healing, I pray also for Your will to be done—understanding that their days are in Your hands. Calm my anxious heart. Hold this one I love so dearly close to you, and bring peace and comfort. Amen.

God, You are my heavenly Father, but my earthly father is a man I love dearly. He cared for me throughout my childhood and teen years, through many hard places, until I grew up and married. He has been there when I needed advice, a good laugh, a hug, a listening ear. Help me face his illness and eventual death with joy, knowing that He will live forever in Your Kingdom, and I will see him again. Amen.

Lord, I feel like I've lost part of myself. I've always known that my mother wouldn't live forever, that someday I would have to face life without her. Still, when the time came, I wasn't ready. I'm afraid I'll forget the sound of her voice, the light in her eyes. Promise me that You will keep her in my heart until the day I see her again. Amen.

DEATH OR ILLNESS OF A PET

"Every animal of the forest is mine,
and the cattle on a thousand hills."
PSALM 50:10 NIV

Dear Lord, some may think this endless stream of tears I'm crying is foolishness—that I'm grieving too deeply over a pet. But Lord, You know and understand the deep connection I've had with my little companion. It feels like I've lost a member of my family. I will miss the unconditional love that has been such a vital part of my life. Comfort my heart, Lord, and help me remember that what we've shared has been a blessing from You. Amen.

Father, I realize that there are many things happening in the world that hold more impact than losing a pet. Just the same, my heart is aching. My sweet girl was both a friend and companion. She brought joy to my life. I don't know how I'll be able to go on without her. I know also that You understand the sadness I'm feeling. Thank You for surrounding me with Your comfort. Amen.

Dear Father, I believe You have concern for every living thing. Not only that, but You are the creator of the animals we cling to so tightly. I pray for the one You have entrusted to me. Oversee his treatment and touch his frail body. Show me how to administer comfort and relief to this animal I have come to love. Amen.

DEATH OR ILLNESS OF A SPOUSE

Just as sin reigned in death, so also grace might reign through righteousness to bring eternal life through Jesus Christ our Lord.
ROMANS 5:21 NIV

Dear God, I'm not sure how to go on living without my soulmate. For so long, it's been "us" walking through life together, hand in hand and heart to heart. You say in Your Word that You are my help in times of need; that You are my friend and confidante. I'm putting my faith and trust in these promises. Thank You for being my comforter and companion. Amen.

Lord, give me strength to stand when things begin to get worse. How can I bear up under all that is required of me? Yet I feel Your hand of comfort, and I know someday I will understand why I had to watch this disease steal life from my sweetheart. Forgive me when I drift into doubt and self-pity. Help me be brave. Amen.

Father in Heaven, I've lost my best friend, my rock. The pain and sorrow are weighing me down to the ground. So much so that I feel I want to die, too. Help me carry this overwhelming burden of grief. Hold me, Lord God, give me strength to walk through this valley of death and come out on the other side singing Your praises. Amen.

DEBT/FINANCIAL STRAIN

"Forgive us our debts, as we also have forgiven our debtors."
MATTHEW 6:12 NRSV

Heavenly Father, help me find a way to resolve the burden of debt that is consuming my life. Where I see no way, guide me to a resolution. I want to be a good steward of everything that passes through my hands, Father. I believe every good and perfect gift is from You, my source of all blessing. Guide my steps as I set goals and priorities for settling and balancing my finances. Amen.

God, it is so easy to spend money and so easy to borrow. Bargains, deals, and more credit card offers come to our home daily. Show us how to resist our material wants, trusting You to supply our material needs. Show us also how to be better managers of the finances You entrust us with. We want to learn to spend and save wisely. Teach us self-control, and help us be better stewards of the money that passes through our hands. Amen.

Lord, my mom and dad are always fighting about money. That's why I try not to ask for anything. Can You help us? Amen.

Father, we need Your help. We've always done our best to manage the money You've given us, but we have been unable to control the hospital bills, the loss of employment, and the many setbacks our circumstances have imposed on us. We need a miracle, Lord—a financial miracle. Thank You for Your promise to provide all we need. Amen.

*As long as I can remember, good people have never been left helpless,
and their children have never gone begging for food.*
PSALM 37:25 CEV

Dear God, everything in my life is being affected by my
financial challenges. Give me real solutions for handling
the daily uncertainty of my current situation. I trust You
as my source and my provider. Give me wisdom and help
me make good decisions. Guide and direct my steps and
actions as I prayerfully work out the details. Amen.

Lord, it is easy to trust You when money is flowing in
and I feel I have plenty. It's easy when no huge expenses
are looming, when no bills are left due, and I'm not in
need. Help me trust You when things are unreasonably
difficult, when my wallet is almost empty, and there is
still a need. Help me trust in Your hand of provision no
matter what the situation might be. Amen.

Thank You, Lord, for wise parents who taught me to
budget my money. It's hard enough to manage even
when I do it right. Amen.

Father, have you forgotten me? It feels that way. The
daily—even hourly—strain of financial shortfalls and
growing debt leave me exhausted and in despair. I ask
You to rise up on my behalf. Speak peace to my heart and
soul as I learn to trust in You. Give me ears to hear Your
wisdom before I act. Amen.

DECEPTION/LYING

Do not be deceived, my beloved.
JAMES 1:16 NRSV

Dear Jesus, someone I trusted has deceived me. I've been trying to process my feelings of brokenness, disbelief, and anger, but I know I need Your healing. The wounded part of me vows to never trust anyone again. And yet, the Holy Spirit in me prompts me to forgive and offer grace. Heal me, Lord. Take this hurt and use it for my good and Your Glory. Amen.

Father, I am afraid that somewhere along the way I might be deceived and tricked, scammed or robbed. I see it daily in the news. Protect me. Help me educate myself so I will not be taken in. Thank you for being there to guide and advise me daily. Keep me watchful yet trusting in You, Lord. Amen.

Dear Lord, I know I've done wrong. Out of selfish pride I've covered up my wrong doing and deceived the very people I love most in the world. Now I feel shame and regret. Forgive me, Lord. Guide me as I work to make amends with those who have been hurt by my deception. Train my heart and mind with the truth, I pray. Amen.

I'm grounded, Lord—again! I don't know why I can't seem to tell the truth. I just do it so my mom and dad won't get mad at me. I know it's wrong. Help me to do better. Amen.

Remove from me the way of lying,
and grant me Your law graciously.
PSALM 119:29 NKJV

Heavenly Father, I know You hate lying of any kind. I don't like being lied to, and I don't want to lie to others. Check my heart and my conscience—that I don't compromise truth. Help me speak truth in love, and help me never lie to myself about what is acceptable to You. Amen.

Father, show me how to teach my children the importance of telling the truth. Amen.

Father, keep my tongue in check. I want to always be honest—always tell the truth. You have called Yourself Truth, and I want to be like You. I want to be faithful and trustworthy. Help me, teach me, and train me to rule over my tongue, to keep it from lies. Remind me to speak honorably and wound my conscience when I don't so that I will only tell truth. Amen.

Father God, it hurts to be lied to. I don't know why people can't just tell the truth. In my hurt I lashed out at the person who lied to me. I was pretty indignant until You reminded me that I have often skirted the edges of the truth myself. Forgive me, Father. Help me while I endeavor to live a more truthful life. Then help me forgive as You have forgiven me. Amen.

DEFEAT/FAILURE

Thanks be to God, who gives us the
victory through our Lord Jesus Christ!
1 CORINTHIANS 15:57 HCSB

Heavenly Father, I know it's not Your will for any of Your children to feel defeated or beat down. You assure us over and over in Your Word that You've provided the way for me to be victorious. You call me an overcomer, and Your Beloved. I cherish these promises, and I will use them to remember that I belong to You, and that You will never leave me to fight my battles alone. Amen.

Lord Jesus, thank You for all the songs and Bible verses that encourage me to keep trying, even when I feel defeat nipping at my heels. The positive reinforcement they bring helps me overcome my own negative thoughts. Thank You for filling my head with lots of reasons to keep going until I succeed. Amen.

Heavenly Father, I have a big test tomorrow. I'm not feeling very confident but I've done the work. Now dad says I need Your help. Thanks God. Amen.

Dear Father, I have come to realize that success often masquerades as defeat. I'm sure Your crucifixion looked like utter defeat to Your disciples. Instead it was the victory of all victories! Show me how to apply this realization to my life. Amen.

The LORD gives me strength. He makes my feet as sure as
those of a deer, and he helps me stand on the mountains.
HABAKKUK 3:19 CEV

Dear Jesus, thank You for Your promise to help me up when I fall, and for empowering me to try again. Keep reminding me that failure is never final; that in You there is always hope and restoration. I lean into You, knowing that even when I fail You, You will never fail me. Amen.

Father, I want to be strong and stable—a person who never messes up, but You, Lord, know my failures. You see my sins and my faults. Thanks for loving and forgiving me. Help me forgive myself. Help me keep trekking on this straight and narrow path that seems often so desperately slippery. Thank You for extending Your hand to help me back up when I fall. Amen.

When You urged me to get up and try again, Lord, I wasn't sure if I could. But with Your help, I did, and this time I made it! Finally, defeat has given way to victory! I give You the glory, Lord. You deserve it all. Amen.

Dear Father, I've failed You so many times, and yet You continue to love and forgive me. My heart is comforted by Your grace and constant, unconditional love. Help me leave my failures behind and walk forward with confidence. Amen.

DELIVERANCE

You are my hiding place; you will protect me from
trouble and surround me with songs of deliverance.
PSALM 32:7 NIV

Father, I think all of us need deliverance from something: sin, sickness, debt, problems, generational curses, our pasts, bitterness, depression, and fears. Whatever it is, Lord, You are the one I will look to. You are the one I know I can trust to be there, ready to help and deliver me. Amen.

Gracious God, deliverance doesn't come easy or without a price. I know it takes a willingness to change and surrender my human will to Your will. The things that hold me captive keep me separated from You. Empty me, deliver me, and free me from everything that divides us. Amen.

Father God, I knew I was skating on thin ice, but I chose to keep going. Now I find myself sinking in an icy sea of presumption and regret. All I can do is reach out to You and pray for a second chance. Deliver me from this mess I've made. Give me an opportunity to do things differently. Amen.

Deliver me, Lord, from the overwhelming constraints of my own schedule and the unrealistic expectations I place on myself. Amen.

DEPRESSION

Answer me quickly, LORD; my spirit fails.
Do not hide your face from me.
PSALM 143:7 NIV

Dear Jesus, it feels as if I've fallen into a dark pit so deep that I can't see or find my way out again. I do believe You love me, that You know where I am and how I got here. Shine the light of Your love as a lighthouse to guide me back to safety and back to You. Change my thoughts to thoughts of hope as I wait for You to rescue me. Amen.

Father, my friend says she has no hope. Help me with the words to show her that everyone has hope in You! Amen.

Lord, help me! A black fog settles down over me, and it is not light or thin. It is dark and heavy, and I just can't seem to push it away. You are my hope in this. Your steadfast love is something I have counted on at other times when depression struck. I commit myself to You, and I know You care. Even the darkness is light to You. Amen.

Sweet Lord, Your light never fails to shine in my darkness. Your love always breaks through my despair. Your faithfulness always dispels my fears. No matter where I find myself, You are there with me. Thank You for Your constant presence. Amen.

DESIRES

Take away my desire to do evil or to join others in doing wrong.
Don't let me eat tasty food with those who do evil.
PSALM 141:4 NCV

Dear Lord, I read that You will give me the desires of my heart. I want those desires to be good and noble and trustworthy. As I pray for what I desire to come to pass, search my heart and let my motives be unselfish and not derived from ego. As the caretaker of my soul, guide my thoughts to desire what will bring Your best plan to my life. Amen.

"I want one of those!" That's what I just heard myself say, Lord. Help me resist being such a wanter. Instead, help me to be a pleaser—someone who pleases You. Amen.

"Reach for the stars," they say. "Go for it! If you dream it, you can do it!" That's what they say, Lord, but maybe it isn't that simple. Maybe You have different plans for me. Maybe You have better plans and realities that are not bubblegum-wrapper wishes. Help me focus my efforts on what You desire for me. Amen.

Heavenly Father, thank You for giving me the desire to do good rather than evil. I thank You also for giving me the power and motivation to live out my good desires while denying the bad. Most of all, I thank You for desiring good things for my life. Amen.

DILIGENCE/LAZINESS

Lazy hands make for poverty, but diligent hands bring wealth.
PROVERBS 10:4 NIV

Father, thanks for reminding me that being diligent
means working hard, but it also means being diligent
to call on You for help when I need it. Thank You for
showing me where my limits lie and sending others to
help get the job done. Amen.

Lord God, I need Your help. All I think about is ministry.
I chide myself for doing too little when the truth is that
I've been diligent to a fault. Show me how to take time
to rest, refresh, and rekindle the flame of passion that
once burned so brightly within me. Teach me to properly
balance diligence with wisdom and understanding so that
I can be all You created me to be. Amen.

Be my coach, Lord. Teach me where I need to be diligent
and where I need to relax and lean on the talents and
skills You've placed in me. Amen.

Father, I think I'm becoming lazy in my relationship
with my spouse. I don't put in the effort any more. Help
me properly value my spouse and never take him for
granted. Amen.

The precious possession of a man is diligence.
PROVERBS 12:27 NASB

Dear God, sometimes I'm too hard on myself. Teach me the difference between a lack of energy, procrastination, and laziness. Strengthen me for the tasks I must complete. Give me the tenacity and motivation to achieve all I need to do with joy and energy. Amen.

Father, forgive me for all the times I have been less than diligent in my faith—not taking time to study the Bible, pray, or meditate on Your Word. Forgive me for taking time to relax when I should've been busy helping the sick, troubled, lonely, hungry, and disabled. I have been slothful in good deeds and service as well. Bless my efforts, Lord, as I begin today to be productive and worthy of living in Your Kingdom. Amen.

At first, I was sure I couldn't do it—too hard. But You kept urging me on, encouraging me to go for it. Now here we are! It wasn't easy, but I did it! Diligence and hard work paid off. Thanks, Lord. Amen.

Lord, I'd like some help motivating my children. Please give me some new and creative strategies. Show me how to teach them the rewards of diligence. Amen.

DISABILITIES

I quit focusing on the handicap and began appreciating the gift.
It was a case of Christ's strength moving in on my weakness.
2 Corinthians 12:9 MSG

Precious Lord, there are things I simply can no longer do. As situations change, I find it harder to adjust to a new way of living with a disability. I do believe good can come from great struggles. Help me mine for the gold in the moments when I have to cope with daily challenges. Help me remember that my life and my weaknesses are made strong in and through You. Amen.

Father, why does my child have this disability? I want him to be whole, complete, and perfect; yet every day he struggles. Why? I know you understand like no one else can. You are the father of many children, and You want wholeness for all of them. Some day ahead You will see us all complete and happy and past our struggles. Then I will see my child well also. Amen.

Lord, nothing has ever been easy for me. Every task is difficult and wrought with frustration and struggle. And yet, I find that I am happy for my life—happy and grateful. Thank You for the life You have given me. Help me glorify You in it each day. Amen.

Father, place in me an empathy for those who battle each day with a disability. Then show me how to reach out and help. Amen.

DISAPPOINTMENT

This hope will never disappoint us, because God has poured
out his love to fill our hearts. He gave us his love through
the Holy Spirit, whom God has given to us.
ROMANS 5:5 NCV

Dear Father, it hurts my heart that something I so
believed in and hoped for didn't come to pass. As I sit
in this empty space of wondering why things didn't
work out, I'm asking You to fill me with renewed hope
and assurance. You have a better plan. Give me peace,
knowing Your plan will replace and far surpass my own
notions of fulfillment. Amen.

Lord, thanks for allowing me to be disappointed again.
I am like a child who wants to eat a whole bowl of
chocolate cake batter, to which You, my loving father,
says "No!" You know me and what I need and don't need.
My foolish soul wants things that aren't good for me, but
You are a good parent. Thanks for saying no to the wrong
things and yes to all the things that are good. Amen.

Father in Heaven, I was so disappointed when things
didn't work out as I'd planned. But now, I see what I
would have missed if my shortsighted plans had worked
out. Maybe someday I will learn to trust You. Someday
I'll learn not to bemoan the good and miss out on the
amazing. Amen.

I may be disappointed in my life at times, but Lord, I
will *never* be disappointed in You! Amen.

DISCIPLESHIP/MENTORING

Others have a gift for caring for God's people as a shepherd does his sheep, leading and teaching them in the ways of God.
EPHESIANS 4:11 TLB

Precious Lord, people cross my path quite often who are in need of spiritual help. Thank You for opening up opportunities for me to mentor those who ask for help and who are seeking more of You and Your light. Make me a good disciple-maker and mentor to those You place in my care. Thank You for trusting me with these hungry hearts. Amen.

Heavenly Father, help me show my friends what it means to follow You. Amen.

Lord, is there someone close by that I have overlooked— someone who needs encouragement, guidance, and advice? Is there someone who has been waiting for You to send a friend, a mentor, a teacher? Is there someone who needs my smile, my voice, and my example? If so, Lord, use me. Someone was there to teach me. Now I want to do the same for someone else. Help me as I strive to be a prayerful mentor— trustworthy and Christlike. Amen.

Father, I have so much to learn about how to live in relationship with You. I ask You to send someone to teach me, guide me, and keep me on track with this beautiful gift I've been given. You've made me Your child, and I want to please You. Send just the right person to help me grow in my faith. Amen.

How I want to follow your orders.
Give me life because of your goodness.
PSALM 119:40 NCV

Dear Jesus, because someone has asked for my help spiritually, expand the desire in my heart to disciple and mentor that person toward a deeper walk with You. Give me wisdom, and the words that will always point to You. Thank You for this opportunity, and thank You for trusting me to plant spiritual seeds of growth in this one who desires to learn and find a deeper relationship with You. Amen.

Lord Jesus, let me be a disciple at Your knee. I want to sit and learn and become wiser and live more like the first twelve who walked with You when You were here on earth. I want to hear Your voice and know it. I want to change and grow to become more like You. When people meet me I want them to say I act and sound and look like You. Amen.

Heavenly Father, I want to be Your disciple. I want to follow You. Amen.

Lord God, You are the great teacher, the Rabbi. As I accept the responsibility to disciple another, I choose to put my own ideas and standards aside, determined to teach about You and only You. I understand the gravity of this assignment. Thank You for placing Your trust in me. Amen.

DIVORCE/SEPARATION

Jesus answered, "Moses gave you permission to divorce your wives because you are so hard to teach. But it was not like that at the time of creation."
MATTHEW 19:8 GNT

Dear God, knowing You are a God of unity, I'm praying for a couple who need a fresh revelation of Your love for them individually and together. Speak life to their marriage and help them see that things have a way of working out if they are willing to work through them with You. Renew their love for each other, and give them a renewed hope for restoration. Amen.

Lord, divorce has become a national epidemic—a plague that has touched each of us. It has brought pain and suffering to my own family. Marriage is such a difficult commitment to make for young people who have had so little experience in life. Now I watch as my own child suffers its scarring effects, and I pray for Your mercy and love to heal us. Restore love and peace in our homes. Amen.

Dear Lord, I never thought that divorce would be a reality in my life. I married for love and for life. And yet, here I am—alone and struggling to deal with the circumstances in my life. I wonder if I will ever be happy again, feel whole again. Help me as I navigate the rocky path ahead. Help me find my way. Amen.

DOUBT

Show mercy toward those who have doubts.
JUDE 1:22 GNT

Dear Jesus, remove the clouds of doubt that are blocking my view. Help me remember that no matter what things look like today, I can believe that good things are on the horizon and faith will rise from the fog. I release my doubts, Jesus, and I'm asking You to rekindle my hope and fill my heart with expectancy again. Amen.

Father, it's easy to say I believe when I sit calmly in church, Bible in my lap, inspiring music enveloping me. I want to have faith when trouble knocks on my door. I want faith when I walk alone, when I am in danger, when I face the incurable and the unfixable. Strengthen me so I never doubt, never flinch, never question Your faithful hand in my life. Amen.

Father God, we human beings are so tied to our senses. Because we can't see or touch You, we doubt. And yet, when I consider the beauty and sophistication of a peacock, count the fingers and toes of a newborn baby, or stare up at the delicate colors of a rainbow, I have no doubt You are real. Thank You for giving me so much to believe in. Amen.

I've never doubted You, Lord, but I often doubt myself. Thanks for reminding me that with Your help I can do anything You ask me to do. Amen.

EDUCATION

*A wise man will hear and increase learning, and a
man of understanding will attain wise counsel.*
PROVERBS 1:5 NKJV

Dear God, I am so grateful for the blessing of education
and what it's brought to my life. You, the source of all
knowledge, present opportunities continually for me to
grow and expand my mind. Keep my mind and heart
always open to learning. Thank You for the discoveries
education brings, and for its limitless and daily
adventure. Amen.

Lord, You framed the universe by knowledge and
wisdom. I wish to have as much knowledge as I can gain
in my life. I don't ever want to stop learning. Encourage
me to keep on in my quest to find new knowledge and
learn new skills. Life's blessings come through these
skills. There is so much I want to learn. Thank you that
the path of education is open to everyone who wants to
take it. Amen.

Father, I pray for the students You have entrusted to my
care. Give them open minds and a hunger for truth. Help
me be worthy of Your trust as I work hard to teach them.
I ask You to help me give them more than math and
science, more than reading and writing. I want to instill
values and self-worth as well. Give me the ability to
grasp new techniques so that I can do the best possible
job. Amen.

EMOTIONAL HEALTH

Get up and pray for help all through the night. Pour out your feelings to the Lord, as you would pour water out of a jug.
LAMENTATIONS 2:19 CEV

Gracious Lord, sometimes I feel that I've landed right in the middle of an emotional windstorm. As thoughts whirl wildly within me, calm my fearful heart and mind. I realize that my overall well-being begins with my ability to control my emotions. As I pray and lay my concerns before You, bring stillness and peace to my mind and my spirit. Amen.

What does it mean when I can't feel You, Lord? Are You still here with me? Amen.

Father, I know of a child who is sick and suffering emotionally, a mother bent down with depression, a father unable to function for no physical reason. Why, Lord? Why? I know You love us. Help me extend heartfelt help to decrease their pain. I look to You for understanding and compassion. Help me love. Amen.

Lord God, I need Your help to set aside my pride and accept the answers You've provided for me. Teach me to look past my shame, past my illness, and past the impulses that I need so desperately to control. I want everything I do to be pleasing to You. Amen.

EMPTY NEST

*I will lie down in peace and sleep, for though
I am alone, O Lord, you will keep me safe.*
PSALM 4:8 TLB

Dear Jesus, I'm not sure I can even describe the emptiness in my heart now that my nest is empty (the nest I've established and nurtured for many years). My role has changed, and the adjustments are difficult. Inspire a renewed purpose in me. As I learn to think and do things differently, remind me that I'm never alone. Fill my heart and home with an abiding sense of Your presence. Amen.

Father, I know You know this pain. You said once how You wanted to gather us like a mother hen gathers her chicks under her wings, but we would not. It's normal and good that our children grow up and go out into the world. Give me the sense to embrace that goodness. Help me offer advice when asked, reserving my pleas and yearnings for prayer. Amen.

It's just the two of us now, Lord—one husband and one wife. What's next? Amen.

Dear Lord, they're all gone and our home feels empty, lifeless. I miss the silly faces and outbursts of joy. Help me through the long days by opening my eyes to opportunities to share my time, gifts, and talents with those outside our home. Amen.

ENCOURAGEMENT

Brothers, rejoice. Become mature, be encouraged, be of the same mind, be at peace, and the God of love and peace will be with you.
2 CORINTHIANS 13:11 HCSB

Dear God, I've often wondered where the encourager goes for encouragement. I'm reminded that David, in the Bible, encouraged himself. I'm not sure how to do that. I love to encourage others, but God, today I'm the one who needs to be lifted up. I look to You for the help I need, knowing You will always be my counselor, my friend, and that You will give me the affirmation I need. Amen.

Thanks, Lord, for smiling on me today! Amen.

Lord Jesus, how fine a small word becomes when it settles into the soul of another—just a "hello," a "bless you," or a "thank you" gives strength. A sentence written in a card or note has helped me go on. May I be the bearer of encouragement to others—those who need a smile and kind word. May I be willing to pitch in and help with cooking, cleaning, babysitting, or sharing someone's burden. Amen.

Father, thank You for the encouragement I find in the scriptures. When I need You most, I find You there, instructing, comforting, affirming, and loving. Any time of the night or day, I go to the Bible and find that I'm refreshed. Thank You for this precious gift. Amen.

ENDURANCE

May you be strengthened with all power, according to
His glorious might, for all endurance and patience, with joy.
COLOSSIANS 1:11 HCSB

Heavenly Father, the race I must run certainly has
become a battle with weariness. Coach me onward,
Father, and give me the strength to persevere, to push
through and press on. When quitting seems easier than
pursuing, keep me focused on the reward that comes
from accepting and appreciating Your ultimate plan.
Amen.

Lord God, endurance isn't needed until I am in a race
and the odds are against me. It isn't endurance until I
have run farther and harder than I think I can. It isn't
endurance until my own inner resources have been
challenged. I have run hard in the past few months; I'm
exhausted. I know there is a prize ahead if I don't give up.
Help me take the next step and the next. Amen.

Lord, help me keep the faith—no matter what! Amen.

Father in heaven, with Your help, I've run the race You've
set before me—but I haven't done it joyfully. Thinking
about it, I don't think I'm capable of being joyful during
times of trouble and trial. I'm sure that would require a
miracle. So I ask, Lord, for a miracle of Your grace. Amen.

ENEMIES

I call upon the LORD, who is worthy to be praised,
and I am saved from my enemies.
PSALM 18:3 ESV

Dear God, there are plenty of enemies to contend with in daily life and in today's society. I may not know how to handle the enemies that come against me on my own, but I know that You do. Thank You for assuring me that no weapon formed against me will ever be successful. I will not fear my enemies because You are my shield of strength as You help me fight each battle. Amen.

Father, I never planned to have enemies. I thought everyone would like me—just because. Turns out I was wrong. There are plenty of people I can't seem to get along with. Teach me to be tolerant of those I disagree with. Show me how to love my enemies. Amen.

Father, crush the enemy of my soul—the evil one who wishes to tear me away from You. Amen.

My Lord, I see in the Bible that You had enemies, but You prayed for them and forgave them. Show me how to love my enemies, pray for those who hate me, and forgive those who are out to do me harm. Amen.

ETERNAL LIFE

The free gift of God is eternal life in Christ Jesus our Lord.
ROMANS 6:23 ESV

Precious Lord, Your gift of eternal life changes the way I look at the trials and griefs I experience in this life. Knowing there's so much more than this earthly life deepens and expands my vision to eternal hope and purpose. Because of eternity's promise, I can live with heavenly expectation and joy. Amen.

Lord, when your friend Lazarus died and his sister came crying, You said, "He is not dead." Those words must have sounded strange since they had wrapped Lazarus in a death cloth and placed him in a grave. Thank You for Your promise of eternal life, and for confirming that promise by raising Lazarus even though his body was decaying. Amen.

Eternity with You, Lord. No beginning and no end! *Amen!*

Precious Lord, I try to imagine what it will be like to live with You for eternity. I simply can't comprehend it. My mind is too small. I do believe though that I will one day live it. Faith will become sight, and I will live in Your presence along with all those who have covenanted with You. What a glorious time that will be! Amen.

EXPECTATIONS

*Shall we not expect far greater glory in these
days when the Holy Spirit is giving life?*
2 Corinthians 3:8 TLB

Dear Jesus, sometimes I'm afraid to believe in good outcomes, better days, and real solutions. If my expectations don't happen as I hope they will, I desperately need the peace and assurance that You still have a plan for my situation. Jesus, in all circumstances of my life, help me remember that my greatest hope and expectation will always be found in You. Amen.

God, my wishes and dreams and hopes have been swept under a rug somewhere. What happened? Were my expectations outside Your will for my life? Was I deemed unworthy to receive them? I may never know the whys and yet I trust You. Teach me to place my hopes in Your expectations rather than my own. Amen.

Your goodness surprises me, Lord. It is so much more than I expected. Amen.

Father God, I have come to believe that I place unrealistic expectations on myself and others. I'm not sure why I do this. I justify these actions in my own mind by saying that I only want what is best for myself and others. As I love and pray and encourage, teach me where the boundaries are between judging and encouraging. Amen.

FACING DEATH

*The law of the Spirit of life has set you free
in Christ Jesus from the law of sin and death.*
ROMANS 8:2 ESV

Gracious Lord, my loved one is facing the final transition from this life into the next. Help me remember that when she takes her last breath on this earth, she will instantly breathe her first breath in heaven. Thank You for Your promise that death is a comma and not a period. Amen.

Lord, my friend is tragically deteriorating and he will not live much longer. It seems so unfair when these things happen to someone so young and beloved. I know You must grieve, too. You are full of compassion. Please send him a miracle of healing. Please provide the help and hope he needs. I know You care, Lord, and that the help of man is futile. Amen.

Father, I am ashamed to admit it, but I'm afraid to die. I believe Your promise of life after death with all my heart, and yet, closing my eyes for the last time terrifies me. Maybe that means I really *don't* believe Your promise. Forgive me, Lord, for my sin of unbelief. Help me grow in faith. Amen.

When I close my eyes in death, Lord, I expect to see only You. Amen.

FAITH

*What I am saying is that we can encourage
each other by the faith that is ours.*
ROMANS 1:12 CEV

Dear Lord, I admit that my faith is not always strong. If I
look at what's before me, those things that look impossible,
my faith feels powerless. Help me remember that You
are working out things behind the scenes of my present
situation. I cannot see in the natural world what You're
doing, but I'm reminded in Your Word that I will see the
evidence that all things are being worked out for my good.
Activate and strengthen my faith with the abundance of
Your promises. Amen.

Father, my faith seems awfully weak lately. I want to be a
person so strong in faith that people whose lives I touch are
healed, restored, fed, empowered, strengthened, and made
joyous. I want to have faith that changes things—faith that
brings results. Now I find myself needing a stronger arm to
hold me. Give me a faith that obeys—a stronger faith—a
powerful faith. Amen.

Dear Father, I've tried placing my faith in earthly things,
human beings, principles and processes, human wisdom
and counsel, human love, and more—but all have failed
me. From this day forward, my faith is firmly centered
in You and only You, for You alone are the never-failing
one. Amen.

I am reaching out to You in faith, heavenly Father. See
me, touch me, heal me. Amen.

FAMILY MEMBERS

Brothers and sisters, since God has shown us great mercy,
I beg you to offer your lives as a living sacrifice to him.
Your offering must be only for God and pleasing to him.
ROMANS 12:1 NCV

Heavenly Father, the concerns for my family members can be all consuming and overwhelming at times. As I pray for my family, help me release and entrust them to Your care. I must remember that Your love for everyone in my family is even greater than my heart can comprehend. Thank You for the blessing of my family. Thank You for Your protection and grace. Amen.

I was once all alone in the world, Father. Thank You for placing me in a family. Now I have a lot of people to love and a lot of people love me. Amen.

Lord, my family is full of needy people. We need You. We need patience, love, faith, hope, and compassion. We need understanding, wisdom, strength, character, and empathy. We need gentleness, self-control, meekness, humility, and temperance in our lives. We all need You. Help us walk with You and improve our character in these days. Lift us higher, Lord. Amen.

Father God, show me how to honor my mother and father. Show me how to respect my sisters and brothers. Help me see each member of my family as a gift from You—yes, Lord, even when they are challenging and difficult. Amen.

FAMILY STRESS

*Make sure that you don't get so absorbed and exhausted
in taking care of all your day-by-day obligations that
you lose track of the time and doze off, oblivious to God.*
ROMANS 13:11 MSG

Father, I feel like I'm running in circles most days,
trying to keep everyone on schedule and meeting their
obligations. Help me keep things in balance, knowing
what You consider to be the priority. Help me be an
example to my family of how to trust You from day to
day. Amen.

Dear God, the stress we feel in our family circle has the
potential for great harm. Personalities, opinions, and
situations seem to quickly change the dynamics of the
peace we all desire. Bring healing, forgiveness, and unity
to the challenges we face as a family. Teach me to be a
peacemaker and peacekeeper. Bless my family with the
covering of Your grace. Amen.

Heavenly Father, help my mom please. She works so hard
to take care of us, and I know she gets tired. Amen.

Lord Jesus, who would know more about the stress in a
family than You do? You walked here on earth, and Your
family suffered not only the daily stress we all feel but
also the stress of knowing, as Mary did, that You were
the Christ who had come to suffer and die for us all.
Help me, Lord, to face my small problems without self-
pity. I know You understand. Amen.

FASTING

It's not too late—GOD's personal Message!—"Come back to me and really mean it! Come fasting and weeping, sorry for your sins!"
JOEL 2:12 MSG

Heavenly Father, when answers don't come, when my prayers seem to hit the ceiling, I need to press in closer to You. Fasting isn't easy, but it gives substance to my faith as I draw near to You and stand firm in my petitions. As I set aside my fleshly needs, help me focus on feeding my faith. Honor and bless my efforts, Father, as I surrender this fasting time to You. Amen.

Lord, I know there are reasons for fasting, but I don't really understand them. I do know it's not about going without food to lose weight. It's not about showing off my "humility" to others. It *is* about giving of my food to hungry people, giving of my comforts to the homeless, giving of my clothing to the naked, and helping to lift burdens from others. It's about putting the needs of others above my own. Amen.

Father, I feel like video games are becoming a problem in my life. Help me put them away for awhile. Amen.

Father, I pray as I set aside time to be with You, that You will purify my body and soul. Whatever form this fasting takes, I ask that You would use it to make me a better person, more eager than ever to seek and obey Your will. Amen.

FEAR

*Even when I go through the darkest valley,
I fear no danger, for You are with me.*
PSALM 23:4 HCSB

Dear Lord, You tell me in Your Word that I am not to fear because You are with me. You tell me that I shouldn't be dismayed because You will strengthen me, help me, and uphold me. Show me how to write those words in my heart. You are my Hero, Lord. The one who answers when I call. The one who rescues me and fights my battles. Replace my fear with faith as I remember who You are and that I belong to You. Amen.

Loving Father, fear is forgetting You are holding my hand. Fear is forgetting I am Your child—forgetting You loved me unto death, quite literally, and even beyond the grave. Fear is assuming You don't care, don't have time for me, aren't out for my best. How can I indulge in fear after You have loved me so? Forgive me. Help me wipe all fear from my heart. Amen.

Dear Father, I see frightened people all around me, people paralyzed by fear, people who have never experienced Your loving care. Help me be loving rather than judgmental. Help me reach out to those around me with a message that the only real fear we should acknowledge is the fear of missing out on a relationship with You. Amen.

FORGIVENESS

Gracious Lord, thank You for forgiving me. It's a gift that I don't deserve. For that reason alone, it should be easy for me to offer forgiveness to others, but so often, it's a real challenge. I can say the words, but I know those words have to be backed by truth and love. Help me remember that when I forgive others, I am passing along a gift that I did not earn. Amen.

Father, the most powerful hurts don't come from strangers. They come from loved ones—my spouse, my children, my parents, sisters, and brothers. Often—too often—they come from those I thought were my dear friends. At times it seems like too much to bear. And yet, I don't want to be locked down and tormented by unforgiveness. Give me the grace to forgive every time, remembering that You have forgiven me. Amen.

Dear Lord, my heart is broken. I need Your forgiveness for my hurtful words and actions. Wipe them away and wash me clean. Help me make it right with those I've offended, and thank You for Your mercy and grace. Amen.

Thank You, Lord, for setting me free. I never could have imagined that forgiveness would feel so good. It's like I'm a new person. Amen.

FREEDOM

*It is for freedom that Christ has set us free. Stand firm, then,
and do not let yourselves be burdened again by a yoke of slavery.*
GALATIANS 5:1 NIV

Dear Jesus, I'm amazed and overjoyed when I think of how You came to ransom and set me free spiritually. You paid the ransom with Your life. Help me never take my earthly freedom for granted, remembering that freedom is never free. Many have paid with their lives. Bless all who give their lives to the defense of freedom, and protect them as they serve and sacrifice. Amen.

Father, thank You for the freedom of heart and spirit that I have found in You. Thanks for freedom from despair and freedom from the bondage of sin. Thanks for the freedom that I could claim even if I were locked in a prison cell. Freedom that cannot be taken from me. Thank You for the freedom that comes from knowing You. Amen.

Lord. I can't imagine what it would be like to be taken against my will and used to satisfy the perverse needs of others. I raise my voice to You, asking for Your help to right this terrible wrong. Show me how I can join the cause to set them free. Amen.

Lord, I'm blessed to serve a God who does not demand my allegiance but allows me the freedom to make my own choice. And I do, dear Father, choose You—today and for the rest of my life. Amen.

FRIENDS

A friend loveth at all times,
and a brother is born for adversity.
PROVERBS 17:17 KJV

Heavenly Father, how do I thank you for the blessing of friendship? You knew that in life's journey, I'd need faithful friends to share my joys and trials. Relationships are precious and true friends are rare. Help me nourish and care for the friends You've given and those I've yet to meet, never taking for granted the blessing of their love. Amen.

Thank You, Lord, for giving me friends who will tell me the truth about myself with love and kindness. Amen.

Lord, my best and closest friends come and go. They love with their best intentions and with effort and strength. They are precious to me, but never can there be an earthly friend who knows me so well and loves me so thoroughly as You do. Thank You, Lord. Amen.

Father, there are those who have loved me well and cared for me often. These friends have been beside me through thick and thin, in good times and bad. They've shared with me their wisdom, and their counsel. They've continued to love me when I was decidedly unlovable. They've comforted me in my pain, and brought light in my times of darkness. Lord, they make me want to be a better friend myself. Thank You for these wonderful people You've placed in my life. Help me be a better friend to each one of them. Amen.

FRUITFULNESS

Walk worthy of the Lord unto all pleasing, being fruitful
in every good work, and increasing in the knowledge of God.
COLOSSIANS 1:10 KJV

Dear God, I want my life to matter. I don't want to serve You with my words only. The true desire of my heart is to serve You and others actively and joyfully. Help me walk in my purpose and calling by bearing good fruit for Your Kingdom. Amen.

Lord, fruit is one of the best foods and the most nourishing. It's harmless and full of flavor and beauty. I want to live a fruitful life, producing much and enriching lives. I want to be fruitful, Lord. Help me become a person who grows and builds and enriches the lives of others—not a user or a taker. Hear my prayer, Father— make my life fruitful. Amen.

Holy Father, the Bible says we are to aspire to the "fruit of the Spirit." From what I understand, that means to grow until I am rich in the attributes of Your Son Jesus. Those characteristics are love, joy, peace, longsuffering, gentleness, goodness, faith, humility, and self-control. Work with me, Lord, to achieve this lofty goal. It's my desire to become a mature tree full of fruit that is pleasing to You. Amen.

Help me remember, Lord, that the fruit of my life will bring nourishment to others long after I'm gone. What joy that brings to my heart. Amen.

FULFILLMENT

He will fulfill what he has planned for me;
that plan is just one of the many he has.
JOB 23:14 GNT

Dear Lord, sometimes, in my search for significance,
I take wrong turns and unsafe detours. I've learned hard
lessons along the way. Among other things, I've learned that
nothing will ever satisfy my heart and soul like Your love
and presence. There are no substitutes for the wholeness
and sense of fulfillment I've found in You. Amen.

Fill me full, Lord—full of joy, peace, love, compassion,
gentleness, goodness, kindness, patience—all the fruit of
Your Spirit. Amen.

Father, I fear that the accomplishments I imagine will
give me fulfillment will instead fall flat without You.
When I examine my dreams closely, I find that they are
mostly temporal and not worth the hopes I have hung on
them. Help me sort them out and replace those that don't
measure up with goals that are truly unselfish—so that I
will find my heart truly fulfilled. Amen.

Lord God, I have set my hope on You. I long for the day
when I will see the fulfillment of Your promises and all
that I read in Your Word has come to pass. Oh the joy that
will fill my heart when I see Your Kingdom established
here on earth, when every prophecy has been fulfilled. I
praise Your name, my Father and my God. Amen.

GENEROSITY

Be generous, and you will be prosperous.
Help others, and you will be helped.
PROVERBS 11:25 GNT

Dear Generous Lord, what a blessing to have been both a recipient of generosity as well as one who has been able to offer it. I clearly see why (in Your Word) "giving" is listed as one of the spiritual gifts. Thank You for the gift of generosity that allows me to bless others and give as You have given to me. Amen.

Father, I want my children to have generous hearts. Show me how to teach and reinforce this powerful lesson. Amen.

Father, teach me to be generous in every part of my life. Teach me to share freely, not only money but my space, time, energy, and possessions. Help me learn to share hope and love, time and experience, joy and grief. Make me generous in all ways—lending a hand, taking time to listen, visiting the sick and lonely, and speaking words of encouragement to those in need of it. Amen.

Dear Father, You could have simply given me life—a chance to walk and talk and breath. That in itself would have been generous beyond measure. But You have done so much more. You died to pay for my transgressions. You've adopted me as Your very own child. You've loved me, cared for me, and immersed me in blessings. Teach me to give of myself to others as You have given of Yourself to me. Amen.

GENTLENESS

Show a gentle attitude toward everyone.
The Lord is coming soon.
PHILIPPIANS 4:5 GNT

Precious Lord, when I become upset or anxious about relationships, it's not always easy to exercise gentleness. Instead of reacting in haste or in anger, help me be more conscious of my attitude and act in a way more characteristic of You. Help me develop a gentle and tranquil spirit that will help me be more at peace within myself. I know I have a lot of growing to do in this area, but my desire is to glorify You in all I say and do. Amen.

I think it's good to be gentle, Lord. Gentle, like when my mom pulls off the bandage after my hurt is better. I want to be gentle like that when I grow up. Amen.

Lord, my own voice startles me sometimes—so course and loud. Help me learn to be a gentle-spirited person— one who people would find approachable and kind-hearted. Teach me to weigh my words, check my volume, and speak as I want to be spoken to. Amen.

Father God, I praise You for Your gentle strength. I see in You the best of both those characteristics. Help me grow more like You each day. Amen.

GOALS

*I keep trying to reach the goal and get the prize for
which God called me through Christ to the life above.*
PHILIPPIANS 3:14 NCV

Dear God, help me understand the difference between
my pursuit of goals and an unhealthy obsession with
them. As I make my plans, guide my actions and steps.
Help my motivations be pure and balanced without the
desperation of competition. Help to always put You first,
God. Let my highest goal always be found in pleasing
You and living in the center of Your will. Amen.

Lord God, what poor goals I set for myself—unreachable
and vague. But the goals I set with Your guidance? That's
another matter. Some of those goals will be difficult;
some may seem quite impossible. The difference is that
I can accomplish any goal when You are helping me,
guiding me, strengthening me, and providing wisdom
and counsel. Thank You, Lord, for making me so much
more than I was. Amen.

Father God, all my life I've been a goal setter and that has
worked well for me. I've achieved much as a result of that
discipline in my life. I've come to see, however, that there
is only one goal that will make an eternal difference—that
is to grow in my relationship with You, learning each day
to be more like You. Help me as I strive to become more
Christlike in all I say and do. Amen.

GOD'S LOVE

I trust in God's unfailing love for ever and ever.
PSALM 52:8 NIV

Dear heavenly Father, love is Your specialty. Love is who and what You are. I stand amazed and in awe that You, the King of kings, Lord of lords, and the Great I Am love me and call me "Beloved." How do I thank You for Your relentless, constant, and unconditional love that never gives up on me? Help me walk worthy of Your love, always in grateful praise. Use me to pour *out* on others the love You've so graciously poured *into* me. Amen.

Father, Your love is immeasurable and true. It does not keep me in a sterile, risk-free place, but enables me to endure hardship and travel rough, uncharted paths. Your love brings out the best in me and urges me to become the person You created me to be. I can't explain Your love for me but revel in it all the same. Amen.

Dear Lord, I feed on Your love. I don't deserve it and I never could. But I do appreciate it and give thanks for it. I do pledge my love to You, as flawed as it might be. Thank You for reaching out to me before I even knew You. Amen.

Until I became a mother, Lord, I had no idea how strong love can be. I'm so glad that You love me like a true father. Amen.

GOD'S PROTECTION

Guard me as you would guard your own eyes.
Hide me in the shadow of your wings.
PSALM 17:8 NLT

Dear God, I'm aware that the enemy of my soul is
constantly waging war against me. I am no match for
him and his minions. I often step into a place of fear
when I feel the battle waging around me. Remind me
daily that You are my shield and my protector. Help me
trust You more and stand on Your promise to defend me
from my enemies. Amen.

Father, You are great and powerful, so powerful that I can
confidently trust in You to keep me safe. Many times I
have been in harm's way, and You have always been there
to protect me. I know there must be count less other
situations when You have looked after me even when I was
unaware of Your saving grace. Thank You for walking with
me through lonesome deserts, dark valleys, and fearsome
places in my life. Amen.

Father God, king David speaks about Your hand of
protection on his life. You kept him safe when he
was chased down and surrounded by those who were
determined to kill him. I can see and feel Your protective
hand on my life, too. Thank You for giving me the same
care You gave those important people in the Bible. Amen.

God, my mom says You will keep me safe especially after
I turn out the light. Thanks. Amen.

GOSSIP

Without wood, a fire will go out,
and without gossip, quarreling will stop.
PROVERBS 26:20 NCV

Gracious Lord, my heart is heavy with regret. I have listened to gossip about someone I care for. Even if I don't speak anything that contributes to the gossip, my listening is still a form of participating. Give me the wisdom and courage to step out of the conversation and speak only healing words of peace. Amen.

Lord, Your words bring life and light and liberty, but words of questionable truth can do great harm. They bring out the worst in us and appeal to our basest nature—pride, malice, and envy. Forgive me when I have indulged in this sinful behavior. Give me a deeper appreciation for the truth, I pray. Amen.

Father, I have seen many damaged by the malicious spreading of untruth. I admit with great sorrow that I have at times engaged in this ungodly practice. Forgive me for this foolishness. I ask You, Lord, to still the lips of the accuser. Cleanse my heart, for I know this has no place in my life. Amen.

Lord, please put a guard on my mouth. It keeps getting me in trouble! Amen.

GOVERNMENT

But our citizenship is in heaven. And we eagerly
await a Savior from there, the Lord Jesus Christ.
PHILIPPIANS 3:20 NIV

Dear God, government issues can be confusing to
people like me who don't always understand how they
work. When I'm called upon to be involved in matters
pertaining to government, I put my trust in You, Lord.
Ruler of heaven and earth, I ask You to ordain and govern
those in leadership. Guide and direct them in faithfulness
to their oaths and responsibilities. Endow them with a
deep desire for honor and stewardship. Amen.

Bless our president, Lord. Give him wisdom, courage, and
humility. Help him guide our country carefully. Amen.

God, You'll come back one day. You won't come as an
infant in a manger, You will come to reign over all the
earth. How great that will be! You as the supreme ruler—
You who has understanding, wisdom, knowledge, grace,
mercy, and compassion. That will be a government I can
trust. Peace will be heard then and every man will find
justice. How I look forward to that coming day! Amen.

Lord in heaven, I pray for my country's governmental
leaders. I pray that You will give them wisdom concerning the affairs of state. Show them how to keep our
nation's citizens safe and free. Amen.

GRACE

The LORD God is a sun and shield: the LORD will
give grace and glory: no good thing will he
withhold from them that walk uprightly.
PSALM 84:11 KJV

Dear heavenly Father, I feel so undeserving of Your grace.
And yet, undeserved favor is exactly how Your grace is
described. Thank You, Lord, for giving me everything
when I deserved nothing. When I was lost, Your grace
found me. Keep finding me, Father. Find me always lost
in Your grace. Amen.

Grace means "unearned favor." I looked it up. I need a lot
of that, Lord. Let Your grace rain on me. Amen.

Lord Jesus, how Your grace precedes, follows, and
envelops me. Help me bestow this gift on those I
encounter each day—even when they don't deserve it.
After all, I certainly don't deserve the favor You've poured
out on me. Let me show grace when someone intrudes
on my space or my plans. Help me show grace when
someone harms or slanders me. I want to give to others
what You've given me. Amen.

Father, I praise You for Your love and grace. Without it,
I would only receive what I deserve, which is less than
nothing. Instead, I have received credit for what Your
Son Jesus has done. Because of Your grace, I am richly
blessed. Amen.

GRADUATION

The wise store up knowledge.
PROVERBS 10:14 NIV

Dear Lord, one day as I watched some baby birds learning to fly for the first time, I was amazed at the process and their progress. Once they were airborne, they had finally graduated. Lord, in all I do, remind me that much effort and perseverance always precedes graduation. Perhaps we're practicing for that one, final, glorious moment when we graduate to our heavenly home. Amen.

Father, graduation is not always a happy event in our lives. We graduate out of situations we love and into harder places. We graduate, but not with the accolades we wished for. We must move on into places and new groups of people and new seasons of life not of our choosing. Help me make it through this "graduation," successfully changing from this phase of life to the next one You have for me. Amen.

Each year, Lord, our young people are launched out into the world unprepared for the spiritual battles they will encounter. Bring some of them to mind so that I can engage in powerful prayer on their behalf. Amen.

Lord God, graduation is as much a beginning as it is an ending. I graduated from high school and began college. I graduated from college and began my career. Not only are graduations a celebration of the past but also a celebration of the future. Thank You for being with me through all the seasons of my life. Amen.

GRATITUDE/THANKFULNESS

Since we receive a kingdom which cannot be shaken,
let us show gratitude, by which we may offer to God
an acceptable service with reverence and awe.
HEBREWS 12:28 NASB

Dear Lord, as I learn the art of gratitude in my daily life, I'm discovering a new kind of power that comes from a grateful perspective. It is giving me a new awareness of every blessing in my life, both great and small. Let me live every moment of every day with gratitude. Amen.

Father, I have so much to be thankful for. Yet I know many times I whine and complain terribly. Help me face every disappointment, troubling circumstance, trial, or shortfall with gratitude. Give me opportunities to show appreciation and take on the habit of being thankful in every situation. A habit is a garment. Make gratitude a *habit* for me—something I wrap myself up in. Amen.

O Lord, sometimes I hear myself saying "thank You" over and over. Words don't seem like nearly enough. Amen.

Holy Father, thank You for loving me, forgiving me, and making me Your child. Thank You for the kindness You show me each day. Thank You for helping me become a better person—one that is pleasing to You. Amen.

Let the peace of Christ rule in your hearts, to which
indeed you were called in one body; and be thankful.
COLOSSIANS 3:15 NASB

Gracious Lord, I'm learning that living a life of thankfulness is more than simply being grateful when something good happens. Even in adversity, blessings arise from the ashes. When I pause in the middle of a busy day and reflect on my blessings, I clearly see that in You, I lack nothing. Give me a thankful heart to live each day as a gift from You. Amen.

Father, I want to use both my words and actions to express my gratitude. Remind me to pause each day to express gratitude to You and to those around me until I have developed a grateful attitude—an aptitude for thankfulness. Amen.

Father, I'm filled with gratitude today. I see Your hand in everything around me. How good it is to be loved and cared for by You! Amen.

Lord, I sense my children need to be grateful for what they have. Like most children, they take so much for granted. Maybe it's time for them to see that others have not been so blessed. I want them to understand that our circumstances are not a gauge of our worthiness. Many others work just as hard for far less. Guide me as I teach them to appreciate and share what they have been given. Amen.

GREED

*Immorality or any impurity or greed must not even
be named among you, as is proper among saints.*
EPHESIANS 5:3 NASB

Dear God, in my pursuit of success and financial security,
give me an open and willing heart to see that all I have is
Yours. Keep me eager to share my bounty and blessings
with others, remembering that You are the source of every
monetary and physical blessing. Amen.

Father, take all wrestling for gain out of my heart. I want
to be a generous and free-hearted person. Give me a
heart to share and give freely. Please root out any seed
of greediness lodged in my heart. Make me more like
Jesus—loving and kind—giving and giving again. Amen.

Lord God, I want more and more and more and more of
You. Amen.

Father, is it wrong to want more than I need or does
greed come into play when I want things for the wrong
reasons? Maybe it's greed when I step on other people to
get what I want or maybe it's when I become consumed
with longing for something like money or power. Teach
me about greed, Lord; how to recognize it and keep it
out of my life. Amen.

GRUDGES

"Do not seek revenge or bear a grudge against anyone among your people, but love your neighbor as yourself. I am the LORD."
LEVITICUS 19:18 NIV

Dear Lord, my energy is drained and my heart is heavy from carrying a rotten old grudge. I should have seen it sooner—the only one I'm hurting is myself. Forgive me for being stubborn and unforgiving. Right now and right here, I surrender this burden to You. Then, Lord, help me leave it with You and never pick it up again. Amen.

Lord, I have a grudge against someone. I've got it gripped so tightly in my sweaty hand that I'm doing harm to myself and others. After all, I can't do anything good until I get my hand back! Help me to let go and forgive fully. Thanks for the sweetness of knowing that You hold no grudge against me. Teach me to love like You do. Amen.

Father God, I've wronged someone and I've never said I'm sorry or even acknowledged the offense. Now each day I'm watching the person I've wronged change before my eyes. She was once optimistic and upbeat, but now she seems dark and unhappy. She's short with others and appears to be angry. If I'm honest, I know why. Give me the courage to acknowledge my wrong and ask her to forgive me. Amen.

Thank You, Lord, for forgiving me freely and refusing to hold my sin against me. Amen.

GUILT/SHAME

*Let us draw near to God with a sincere heart and
with the full assurance that faith brings, having our
hearts sprinkled to cleanse us from a guilty conscience
and having our bodies washed with pure water.*
HEBREWS 10:22 NIV

Dear Jesus, my guilt is often self-inflicted and keeps
me trapped in a prison of my own making. One of the
hardest things to grasp in my mind and heart is how to
truly forgive myself. Help me accept the forgiveness You
give, remembering that if You forgive me, I have no right
to do less. Help me release all guilt and shame to You,
and leave it at Your feet. Amen.

Father, I am swimming in guilt, and it feels like I'm
going under for the last time. The current is swift, and
I am weak. Save me from the horrible power of guilt,
whether earned or imagined. I lay my sins and failures at
Your feet and, once again, confess my regret and sorrow.
Save me, Lord. Amen.

Lord God, I've done it again. I've used guilt to
manipulate someone. Of course, it ended badly as it
always does. And the worst part is that I know this tactic
is not pleasing to You and causes resentment. Even
though my desires for others come from a pure heart,
that doesn't justify my tactics. Teach me to speak truth
and then leave it in Your hands. Amen.

Take away the shame I fear, because your laws are good.
PSALM 119:39 NCV

Dear God, it's not Your nature to shame us, but I certainly feel ashamed. In a fit of emotion, I let my guard down and pushed my way into a situation where I didn't belong. I'm ashamed of myself. I see the mess I've caused. Forgive me, Lord. Show me what I can do to make it right. Thank You for taking away my shame. Amen.

Dear Father, I stood up from prayer with a new heart, a grateful heart. My shame is gone. You have made me clean and white as snow. My enemy can no longer accuse me because You have declared my debt paid. Now, Lord, I stand before You and declare my love for You, my Savior and my God. Amen.

When my enemies try to shame and bully me, I am not afraid because I know how much I mean to You. Amen.

Lord, thank You for the opportunity to work with these beautiful children. I understand the responsibility You have entrusted to me. I pray that I will never bring shame on them. Protect them from cutting words spoken in haste or anger. Let me teach them with love and with an understanding of their fragility and their sweetness. Help me always be kind and encouraging, even when they misbehave. Amen.

HEALING

*For you that honor my name, victory will
shine like the sun with healing in its rays.*
MALACHI 4:2 CEV

Dear God, You are my Healer. Your Word tells me that
You paid for my healing with the pain and suffering You
experienced on the cross. When I'm hurting, when I
need Your hand to touch me and make me whole, help
me ask and then wait before You. I will not demand. I
will not beg. Instead, I put my life completely in Your
hands. Amen.

Father, You are a physician, but not one like we know
here on earth. You are the one who created us and You
know us in ways that no other physician possibly could.
I look to You for wholeness—healing in my body, mind,
soul. I've received Your healing touch in the past, and I
know its transforming power. Help me as I surrender
myself to You and trust You to make me whole. Amen.

I praise You with my whole heart, my healer and my
God. Amen.

Lord, You are the Great Physician. I have great
confidence when I come before You and ask for healing
because You created me and You know every cell of my
body, every thought in my mind, every cry of my heart.
Thank You for Your gift of healing. Amen.

HEAVEN

*Rejoice and be glad, because you have a great
reward waiting for you in heaven.*
MATTHEW 5:12 NCV

Dear heavenly Father, I believe I was born with this
longing in my heart that can never be filled here on
earth. I look forward to the place You've prepared that
is far greater than I can imagine. It's also a comforting
thought when those I love pass from this earth and go to
live with You. Thank You, Father, for the promise of my
heavenly home. Amen.

I close my eyes, Lord, and try to imagine what heaven
will be like. But it's too much for me. I guess I'll have to
wait and see. Amen.

Lord Jesus, I look forward to the day when heaven will
come down, and we will be together with You forever.
So many men and women have imagined heaven and
have ideas and beliefs about what it's like. I know only
that it is a good place and I want to be there. You will
be there and no matter what else, that will make it truly
wonderful. Amen.

Father, I long for heaven. I long for Your promise of
eternity spent in Your presence. I long to see the place
You have prepared for me. I long to see my loved ones
who have gone before me. I long to forever be drenched
in the light of Your love. I praise You for Your great and
magnificent promises. Amen.

HELPLESSNESS

When he saw the crowds, he had compassion for them, because
they were harassed and helpless, like sheep without a shepherd.
MATTHEW 9:36 ESV

Precious Lord, You've promised never to leave me in
my times of need. Your Word says that You will be my
ever-present help when I'm overwhelmed. Hear the cries
of my heart, Lord. Replace my helplessness with seeds
of hope in Your Almighty power. Help them grow and
bloom and take root deep in the soil of my spirit. Turn
my dark days of helplessness into light-filled days of
victory. Amen.

Lord Jesus, I see many around who feel desperate and
helpless. They don't know that You are a God who
specializes in the impossible. Nor do they know that they
can safely trust You with their deepest hurts and find
healing. Make me an encouragement to them—always
ready to give the reasons for the hope in my heart. Let
me point souls struggling on the edge to You. Amen.

Father God, I've never felt so completely out of control.
And yet, I know I can turn to You for help. Forgive me,
Lord, for trusting in myself, refusing Your guidance, and
going my own way. Distance me from those things that
brought me to this place and left me sinking into the
quicksand below my feet. Pull me up onto solid ground
I pray, and save me from my defiant and disobedient
ways. Amen.

HIDDEN SIN

God shows his love for us in that while
we were still sinners, Christ died for us.
ROMANS 5:8 ESV

Dear God, there are things in all of our lives that we
keep tucked away in the secret chambers of our hearts.
But whether small or great, nothing is hidden from You,
God. Shine the light of the Holy Spirit on my heart and
expose every hidden sin that needs to be surrendered and
forgiven. Keep my heart open and truthful with a No
VACANCY sign to secret sin. Amen.

God, I have hidden my sin from everyone—except You.
I know that nothing I do is hidden from Your eyes and
nothing I say is hidden from Your ears. I seek Your
forgiveness and thank You once again for Your grace.
I'm very sorry for my deceit and deeply grateful for Your
mercy. Amen.

Know me just as I am, Lord. Nothing is hidden from
You. Amen.

Holy Father, once again I have dug a hole for myself—
a hole so deep I have no hope of pulling myself out of
it. Everyone who hears of my sin will be shocked and
disappointed. They will all know that I'm not the person
they thought I was. Give me the courage to confess my
sin and live with the consequences. Amen.

HOLINESS

*May your hearts be made strong so that you will be
holy and without fault before our God and Father
when our Lord Jesus comes with all his holy ones.*
1 THESSALONIANS 3:13 NCV

Heavenly Father, the closer I draw to You, the more I
am filled with Your presence and the wonder of Your
holiness. Help me declutter everything in my heart and
spirit that keeps me from being holy as You are holy.
Show me those places where I fall short. I know I will
never be completely holy in this life, but thank You for
calling me holy because I have been cleansed by Your
blood. Amen.

God, not much is considered holy or sacred in our world
today. There are people who scoff at Your name and make
fun of Your Word. I am sorry that things have gotten
so bad, and I pray that we would be convicted of this
and renewed in our understanding of Your purity and
holiness. Amen.

Dear Father, if holiness means completely clean and
sinless, I know I will never achieve it. No matter how
I try, I can never walk in full holiness. Help me walk
before You, asking for Your forgiveness as soon as my
sinful nature steps in. This is indeed a high calling for
which I must count on You completely. Amen.

HOLY SPIRIT

*"The Helper, the Holy Spirit, whom the Father will
send in my name, will teach you everything and
make you remember all that I have told you."*
JOHN 14:26 GNT

Dear Jesus, after you lived on this earth as God's Son,
You left the priceless gift of the Holy Spirit here to help,
instruct, and comfort me. I'm learning to depend on the
Holy Spirit as my helper and constant companion in my
everyday walk with You. Thank You for this indescribable
gift. Amen.

God, You are indeed a holy spirit. I too am a spirit, but
not holy. I live inside my human body and possess a
soul. Here my troubles begin! I want to be holy like You
are, Father, but I have so much to overcome. Thank You
for loving and receiving me in my ruined state, always
forgiving and showing me how to walk in a way that is
pleasing to You. Amen.

Father: Your Holy Spirit is great and powerful. He is Your
presence living inside me, helping me do my best and
encouraging, instructing, and inspiring me to become the
person You created me to be. It's an honor to have You in
my life. Show me how to make my heart a place where
You can enjoy residing. Amen.

Come fill me, Holy Spirit. I want more and more of You.
Amen.

HOME

*Through [skillful and godly] wisdom a house [a life, a home,
a family] is built, and by understanding it is established
[on a sound and good foundation].*

PROVERBS 24:3 AMP

Dear God, one of my greatest blessings is my home. Not
only does it provide shelter for me and my family, but it's
my safe place of physical rest and love. I'm grateful that
in this place Your presence also dwells. Help me always
care for my home with a spirit of gratitude, never taking
Your provision for granted. Amen.

Father, I've never had a home of my own. I've lived in
foster homes, with relatives, in apartments, hotels, shelters.
For a while I lived in my car. Sometimes I wonder what
it would be like to live in one place for more than a few
months, to have my own bed and feel comfortable and
settled. You've been there with me, but I long for a place to
call my own. Thank You for hearing me, Lord. I have no
one to talk to but You. Amen.

Heavenly Father, I find myself so far from home and all
that is familiar. I know I'm doing what You have called
me to do, but my heart still longs to be in the midst of
family and friends. It's not so much the place as it is the
people that I miss. Comfort my heart tonight, Lord.
Help me stay focused on the task at hand. Amen.

HONESTY/DISHONESTY

If you do the right thing, honesty will be your guide.
PROVERBS 11:3 CEV

Heavenly Father, as much as I admire the attribute of honesty, I find, at times, that there is a thin line between honesty and compromise. I've encountered compromising actions from others but I've also discovered that thin line can be blurred by circumstances and my own reactions to them. Keep check over the motives of my heart. Help me remain honest in character and always true to my convictions. Amen.

Lord, since I was a small child, I have been taught the virtue of honesty. Yet sometimes I find myself shaping and polishing little half-truths. The trauma of finding myself caught in one of these is disturbing. Am I really capable of calling them what they truly are—lies? My heart scolds me. My conscience is in distress. Save me, Lord. Teach me to be perfectly and ever honest. Amen.

My teacher says, "honesty is the best policy." I'm pretty sure she got that from the Bible! Amen.

Lord in heaven, it hurts to know someone I care about has failed to be honest with me. I feel dishonored and betrayed. This is how You must feel when I'm not honest with You. Help me guard my tongue against dishonesty in every form—words, thoughts, and actions. And help me forgive the dishonesty in others as You have forgiven the dishonesty in me. Amen.

Who may climb the mountain of the Lord and enter where he lives?
Who may stand before the Lord? Only those with pure hands and
hearts, who do not practice dishonesty and lying.
PSALM 24:3–4 TLB

Dear Lord, I've come across a situation of dishonesty
that I know must be addressed. My heart is torn as
I ponder how to confront something so delicate,
something I know can only be dealt with by Your grace.
Dishonesty leads away from You and compromises
everything we say we believe. Allow the Holy Spirit to
convict and bring repentance to hearts and lives. Amen.

Dear God, forgive me for not being as honest as I should
be. Change me on the inside so that I will be truthful
and honest in all I say. Let my actions speak truth. Let
my written words ring true. May even my words to
myself be frank and forthright. Scald me with regret
when I speak white lies and half-truths or use truth to
deceive someone. Cure me of dishonesty, I pray. Amen.

There are so many voices out there, Lord. Give me
discernment to know the truth when I hear it. Amen.

Lord, You expect good things, honest things, pure things
from those who follow You. Wash me clean of wrong
doing. Clear my thoughts and words of deceit and
dishonesty. Help me live honestly, confirming Your trust
in me. Amen.

HONOR

Wait for the Lord's help and follow him.
He will honor you and give you the land.
PSALM 37:34 ICB

Dear Lord, honoring You and honoring people is a primary choice and vital part of all I want to be. Your Word is clear about putting You first in my life and honoring You with all my heart. I know that honoring You is part of loving You. And honoring others is essential to loving them. Give me a selfless kind of humility that strives to be honorable and respectful in my words and deeds. Amen.

Lord, when is honor ever due a man? Shouldn't honor go only to You? I guess not, because Your Word teaches us to honor our parents, those in authority over us, and our spouses. Seems we often honor unworthy persons, like celebrities and athletes, or we seek honor for ourselves. Teach us about honor—how and when to show it to others. May we live to honor You. Amen.

Father, I ask You this morning to pour out honor on those who are fighting for our country, those who are fighting in foreign countries on behalf of the Gospel, and those who fight here in our country to keep the peace and protect our nation's citizens. I ask You to defend them and keep them out of harm's way. Amen.

Help me honor my mom and dad, Lord. That means "obey," right? Amen.

HOPE/HOPELESSNESS

There is a future, and your hope will not be cut off.
PROVERBS 23:18 NRSV

Dear Lord, help me remember that because of You and through You, hope always exists. Even in the hard places of my life when I'm feeling desperate, I'm believing that Your empowering hope will rise up in me. Though unseen, hope is always near because of Your Spirit that dwells in me. You are always listening, always caring, and always steadying my heart and my steps. Amen.

Father, in my situation, hope seems to be a cruel joke. The diagnosis is bad. The prognosis no better. There's nothing left to hope for—at least that's how it seems. Let me see the picture from Your viewpoint. Help me find a ray of sunshine—not small and waning but bright and marvelous. Hope is what I really need. Speak peace to my heart. Help me trust. Help me hope. Amen.

I'm only helpless, Lord, when I don't place my hope in You. I never want to do that. Amen.

Lord God, I placed my hope in You in my very darkest hour, and You did not disappoint me. Instead, You eased my fear and came through for me in a big way. It wasn't the way I pictured it, but it anchored my trust in You and gave me back my future. Thank You with all my heart. Amen.

O God of our salvation, You who are the trust and hope
of all the ends of the earth and of the farthest sea.
PSALM 65:5 AMP

Gracious Lord, feeling stuck and helpless in my situation brings me to the end of my own resources. Change my thoughts of discouragement to believing in, relying on, and knowing You are working out every victorious detail in my life. Amen.

God, so many in the world today live in poverty and war. But when I look at photos of foreign children, I see hope rather than hopelessness. I see smiles. Maybe these are staged; I wouldn't know. What I do know is that You are the God who is near, and the God who is far away. You live and love in places I would consider hopeless. Thank You for Your universal presence and for the gift of hope for people everywhere. Amen.

Father, my situation seems to have no solution—at all! I've prayed and prayed but so far nothing has changed. My friends tell me to give up—You aren't listening. But I don't believe that. I know You hear me, and You are working on my behalf. I know You are able to change the most hopeless situation into a bright victory. Give me courage and patience as I wait on You to transform the impossible into the possible. Amen.

HOSPITALITY

Be quick to give a meal to the hungry,
a bed to the homeless—cheerfully.
1 PETER 4:10 MSG

Thanks for welcoming me into Your family, Lord. Amen.

Dear God, whenever I open my home or my heart,
I've sensed Your presence and Your Spirit of love. I
believe others sense it, too. Thank You for the gift of
hospitality. Help me serve others with the joy of Your
love extended. Amen.

Father, open the doors of my house and also the doors of
my heart. Help me show hospitality in my home, my life,
my circumstances, my emotions—in all the places that
I label mine. Of privacy and invasion—invasion may be
the better thing. Help me hold the doors of my life wide
and offer help, hope, and blessing to all You send my way.
Cure me of selfishness, Lord. Amen.

Lord, I've got a problem and I know it. I don't like
people touching my things or invading my space. But
lately I've been thinking. What if You hadn't invited me
to share Your space? What if You had been too selfish to
be hospitable to me? Help me reach out to others just as
You have reached out to me. Amen.

HUMILITY

Dress in the wardrobe God picked out for you:
compassion, kindness, humility, quiet strength, discipline.
Colossians 3:12 MSG

Gracious Lord, because of my accomplishments, it's easy to let pride slip into my thoughts. I need humility to keep my heart and motives in check. You are my source, Lord; and all good gifts come from You. Help me work and serve with a humble attitude and from a fully surrendered heart, always for Your glory. Amen.

Father, if I deem myself spiritual, I am certain You know better. I am silly to think You are fooled by my pretense. Everyone else will surely see through me as well. Even I know the truth. I am faulty and weak. Teach me to live humbly—not in a downcast, face-to-the-ground manner, but in the humility of fully knowing who I am and who You are. Amen.

Father God, I'm a shy person. I don't draw attention to myself or say prideful things. For a long time, I thought that was humility. Now I know that's just another way of putting myself before others. Thanks for opening my eyes to my pridefulness. Teach me true humility, Lord. Come to think of it, it probably won't be an easy or pleasant lesson. But it's my desire to be more like You. Amen.

Sometimes, Lord, when I pray for humility, I hope You won't answer me. Amen.

HUNGER, SPIRITUAL

Hunger is good—if it makes you work to satisfy it!
PROVERBS 16:26 TLB

Dear God, the more I seek You, the more I find You. This hunger I feel to know You more—I don't want it to ever end. As I read Your Word, feed my spirit and my mind with Your wisdom. I'm asking the Holy Spirit to help me understand all that I read with a greater measure of clarity. Draw me nearer to You, God. Fill my heart and life with Your presence. Amen.

O Lord, I long to know You. Let me know that You're real. Amen.

Lord Jesus, we are hungry for Your words and Your presence. We are hungry to visit with You. Come closer and remember, Lord, how we are made of dust—hungry, shortsighted, foolish people. Yes, come closer and fill up our spiritual reservoirs with living water and our soul's gardens with food that will nourish us and cause us to grow and thrive. Amen.

God, my physical hunger is always there. Like most people, I feed it much too often. But my spiritual hunger—that I tend to ignore. My soul must be thin and puny. Give me a hunger for spiritual things, a ravenous hunger like I had when I first knew You. I'll begin with the food You've provided in Your Word, the Bible. Open my eyes to see and desire the bounty You've left for me there. Amen.

HUNGER, PHYSICAL

Who shall separate us from the love of Christ?
Shall trouble or hardship or persecution or
famine or nakedness or danger or sword?
ROMANS 8:35 NIV

Dear Lord, there are times when my physical hunger
stems from being exhausted or anxious. I've become
aware during these times that I make wrong choices for
my physical well-being. When I'm hungry, help me take
the time to pause and give thought to what will nourish
me physically. We are spirit, mind, and body. Make me
mindful of the strengths and weaknesses of my hunger so
I will take better physical care of myself. Amen.

I was hungry, Lord. We all were. We prayed and asked
You to send us some groceries. Dad said You would
take care of us. When the doorbell rang, we wondered
who it was. A nice man and woman brought us bags of
groceries, enough to last for a long time. They said You
told them to. Now I know You really care. Thank You so
much for hearing us when we prayed! Amen.

Father, across our nation there are families with empty
pantries and empty pockets. I know they are asking You
for help. I would in their place. Use me, Lord. Let me
be part of the answer for these precious children and
worried parents. You have blessed me with more than
I could ever need. I'm going to reach out. Lead me to
those who are in need. Amen.

IDOLS

Little children, keep yourselves from idols.
1 JOHN 5:21 KJV

Dearest Lord, I see that so many things can easily become idols in my life—tangible things owned, dreams, my career, and even the people I love. These are all good blessings gifted by You. They become idols only when I give them the place You should occupy foremost in my heart. As Lord of my life, examine my heart and help me put You first. Amen.

Oh Lord, You will always be first with me. Amen.

Lord, they call them statues in the museum—small metal, clay, or wood figures that men have worshipped. I call them idols and abhor them. Still, I know that there may be idols in my life that I don't recognize as such. Examine my heart, Lord. Make me aware of anyone or anything I trust in or worship rather than You. I want to worship You alone. Amen.

Father, how it must hurt You when I put other things before You. I don't mean to allow those distractions to come in—but I open the door and soon my focus, my interest, and even my devotion has drifted away from You. I wish my idols were made of wood and stone. Then I could just throw them away once and for all. But instead, they are standing tall in my heart and mind. Thank You for helping me drag them down and cast them out forever. Amen.

INFERTILITY

*He makes the barren woman abide in the house
as a joyful mother of children. Praise the LORD!*
PSALM 113:9 NASB

Dear heavenly Father, I'm ashamed to say I'm jealous. I'm happy for my friends. Their dream of having a child is coming true. But…we're still waiting. Banish my jealous feelings and replace them with honor for Your plan and purpose. Remind me often that You are perfecting all that concerns me and making all things beautiful in Your time. Amen.

Dear Jesus, a dear couple I love sincerely desires to have a child of their own. I pray this desire will come to pass. You know best how everything will work out for their good, in ways we may not see right now. According to Your perfect will, fulfill this desire through the unfolding of Your plan in their lives. Amen.

Lord, no matter what, thank You for always knowing what's best for me. Amen.

Father of All, I thought I would never be a mother. I felt that I had love enough for twenty babies—yet my arms remained empty. Then I saw it. A mother's heart is a caring heart and there are so many who need to be cared for. I reached out and the emptiness inside began to disappear. Thank You, Lord, for choosing me for this special ministry. Thank You for allowing me to love the unlovable and mother the motherless. Amen.

INHERITANCE

*Giving thanks to the Father, who has qualified us
to share in the inheritance of the saints in Light.*
COLOSSIANS 1:12 NASB

Dear God, as Your child, I have been given access to all
You've promised. Like a gift that remains unwrapped,
I will never know the power of my inheritance until I
claim it. Thank You, God, for the richness and wonder
inherent in all Your gifts. Amen.

O Lord, I fear for nothing because I have inherited all
Your promises. Amen.

God, the Bible says that a good parent leaves an
inheritance for his children. My mother left me with
so many treasures—treasures like courage and a can-
do attitude, compassion, and an eye to see the world's
beauty. The things she passed into my hands are things
no money can buy. May I be faithful to leave such an
inheritance for my children. Amen.

Father, so many of my friends received an inheritance
from their parents, a nest egg to buy a first home or
fund a much-needed vacation. My parents were good
people. They gave me a great deal, just not in monetary
form. They gave me their love, their values, and most of
all, their faith. They introduced me to You when I was
just a child. They taught me from the Bible and showed
their faith in the way they lived. Thank You for such a
powerful inheritance. Amen.

INSOMNIA

He gives sleep to His beloved.
PSALM 127:2 NRSV

Dear Lord, most nights, when I close my eyes, my mind races and rewinds the concerns of my day and the obligations I face tomorrow. I wonder how everything will be accomplished. Lord, help me relax and breathe in Your peace. Help me surrender my anxiety and worries to You. Heal every emotional and physical condition that is troubling me. As I close my eyes, cover me in the warmth of Your assuring presence. Amen.

Lord, I can't rest. My mind is bouncing from one problem to another, trying to extract a solution. In the end, the exercise is completely unproductive. I get up in the morning exhausted and still carrying my burdens. Thank You, Lord, for Your promise of sleep. I ask You to reprogram my troubled mind by dismissing each problem that bounces up with the assurance that You are the great problem solver. Thank You for Your blessings. Amen.

Father God, I need sleep, but my body won't cooperate. I feel every ache and pain. My heart races and my arms and legs refuse to relax. The Bible says that sleep is a blessing, a gift. Each night, I have determined to see myself unwrapping that gift from You as I slip beneath the covers. It's just a gesture, Lord; it has no power in itself. I trust You to make Your promise real as I reach out in faith. Amen.

INTEGRITY

The righteous man walks in his integrity;
his children are blessed after him.
PROVERBS 20:7 NKJV

Heavenly Father, integrity is the mark of true moral character, and a quality I deeply desire. Condition my heart and spirit to always take the high road. In my everyday living and choices, help me live honestly and uprightly before You and in relationship with others. Amen.

Lord Above, help me walk in truth and integrity by reinforcing my conscience. Amen.

Father, I heard a child say of his parents that they acted the same at home as they acted when others were watching. My first response was, "Don't we all"? Then I asked myself these questions: "Am I honest when no one sees?" "Do I do the right thing regardless of the circumstances?" "Is my word my bond?" "Do my children recognize me in public?" We both know what my answers to those questions are, Lord. Help me grow in integrity, I pray. Amen.

Lord in heaven, I find it easy to follow the changing values the world espouses, and I often forget that the issues of right and wrong are concrete. They don't change. I ask You to help me grow stronger in my convictions. Amen.

JEALOUSY

I fear that some of you may be arguing or jealous or angry or selfish or gossiping or insulting each other.
2 CORINTHIANS 12:20 CEV

Father, the Bible says You are a jealous God. That had me stumped until I realized that Your jealousy is only for our good. It's a love thing. You don't want us running after false gods—things that will keep us from relationship with You, our Creator, and steal all the blessings You have intended for us. That makes me feel so loved. Thank You, Lord, for caring so deeply. Amen.

My sister gets all the best stuff, Lord. Mom and Dad just love her more than me. Why? Amen.

Lord, forgive me for exhibiting the kind of jealousy that is sinful in Your eyes—the selfish kind, the kind that wants what others have. Cleanse me, Lord, and help me be grateful for what I have, which is so much more than I deserve. Amen.

Father, help me instill in my children a strong sense of worth so that they won't be subject to the green-eyed monster: jealousy. I want them to know You created each of them with the same loving care. The clothes we wear, the possessions we attain are all just window dressing. This is a tough job. Give me wisdom, Lord, so I can teach these precious children You've given me. Amen.

JESUS' RETURN

"If I go and prepare a place for you, I will come again and will take you to myself, so that where I am, there you may be also."
JOHN 14:3 NRSV

Dear Jesus, Your return can't come soon enough for this world. As earthly conditions decline on all levels, You have not left us hopeless. You are our hope and our King who has promised to make all things new. In the meantime, help me fulfill my Kingdom purpose, and help me joyfully share the promise and expectation of Your return with others. Amen.

Come quickly, Lord Jesus. My heart longs for You. Amen.

Lord Jesus, I look for the day of Your return. On that day, I will see You with my eyes as You rule in righteousness and reign in justice. No longer will we be subject to the governments of the world. We will be Your people and Yours alone. Until that day, I wait patiently. Come soon. Amen.

Father, thank You for Your promise to come back for me and all those who love and honor You. What a day that will be. I worry and fuss over the details of this life, forgetting that our days here are by no means the end. We have a bright future with You. Amen.

JOB LOSS/JOB STRESS

I have been young, and now am old, yet I have not seen
the righteous forsaken or their children begging bread.
PSALM 37:25 NRSV

Dear Jesus, my friend suddenly lost her job and source of income. She is devastated and can't imagine how she will manage her responsibilities without employment. Bring relief and peace to her heart as she waits for Your guidance. Give her wisdom as she takes her next step forward. Help her see that this setback is a stepping stone to something better You have planned for her future. Amen.

Lord, I know it's difficult to be out of work. I've been there myself. You worry about the bills. Your self-esteem plummets. You wonder how You'll ever catch up even if You do find someone willing to take a chance on you. Help those who are without work. Give them courage to apply and patience to wait. Until the right job opens up, cover their needs with Your bounty. Amen.

Father, I lost my job today. I know it's not the end of the world, but it sure feels like it. Along with all the other emotions, I feel a certain level of rejection and confusion. Where do I start to get back on track? I need guidance, Lord, and favor with employers. I need provision for my family, and grace to see us through the tough times ahead. Thank You for Your promise never to forsake us. Amen.

Commit your work to the LORD,
and your plans will be established.
PROVERBS 16:3 NRSV

Dear Lord, my job is robbing me of my peace and well-being. None of these conditions line up with Your will or desire for me. Show me how to manage the stress my job brings to my life. Rather than handling and accepting the stress, help me do my part to alleviate it, praying, reacting, and responding with peace. Amen.

One day at a time, Lord. Help me take just one day at a time. Amen.

Father, I'm a mother and I work hard. I'm on call twenty-four hours a day, seven days a week. I'm expected to keep my house in perfect order and prepare hot meals. My job description is a joke—nurse, teacher, chauffeur, scheduler, childcare specialist, to name just a few. Half the time I don't know if I'm coming or going. Don't get me wrong, I love my husband and children, but I need some relief. I commit my situation to You, Lord. Help me do the best for my family without sacrificing my well-being along the way. Amen.

Father God, I thank You for my job. It isn't glamorous or exciting, but it allows me to pay the bills and take care of my family. Help me remain grateful for what You've given me by turning to You with any stressors, unfair treatment, frustrations, and conflicts. I believe You will always deal generously with me. Amen.

JOY

I will sing for joy about what your hands have done.
PSALM 92:4 NCV

Dear God, thank You for teaching me the difference between joy and happiness. Circumstances cannot steal the steady, abiding joy I find in You. While happiness depends on the ever-changing conditions of my life, Your joy, flowing freely through me, is part of my constant oneness with You, God. Amen.

Lord God, the words of the Sunday school song I learned as a child remind me that Your joy is *down in my heart to stay*! Amen.

Lord, it isn't easy to be cheerful and happy in the hard spots of life. Some times are downright terrible. Still, I have Your joy—the constant knowing that I belong to You and You love and care for me. Joy springs up and floods over me when I remember Your faithfulness. Amen.

My Lord, the circumstances of life have weighed me down and stolen my joy. I remember how it was when I first gave myself to You. I couldn't contain my happiness. My joy bubbled up constantly. But now I've let it slip away. I have so much to be joyful about, so much to thank You for. Ignite the flame in me once again. Help me push out the fears and fatigue and praise You once again with a joyful heart. Amen.

JUDGING

"Don't judge others, or you will be judged."
MATTHEW 7:1 NCV

Gracious Lord, I really hate it when people judge me. I once heard someone say that people may forget the things you say or do, but they will never forget how you make them feel. Lord, quicken my heart when my attitude becomes judgmental or condemning. Help me see others through Your eyes. Give me a nonjudgmental heart of grace, remembering how much I've been given. Amen.

Father, if I judge others at all, it should be with the same yardstick I want to be judged with—fairly and without hypocrisy. You are strong and powerful and perfect in all of Your ways, and You judge with empathy and compassion. Instead of judging others, help me lend a helping hand. Teach me how to be an advocate rather than a critic. Amen.

Lord, I have judged myself to be unworthy of Your love. You have judged me to be pleasing in Your sight. I have judged myself to be guilty of trespasses and sins. You have judged me to be clean and forgiven. I have judged myself to be without hope. You have judged me to be full of hope. Thank You for seeing me not as I was but as I am through the sacrifice Jesus has made for me. Amen.

Lord, I'm so glad You are the great judge—You and no one else. Amen.

JUSTICE/INJUSTICE

"He [God] will persist until he causes justice to triumph."
MATTHEW 12:20 GNT

Dear Jesus, sometimes it seems there is no real justice in this life. It's often so tempting to take matters into our own hands. Your Word reminds me that You are the vindicator and justifier. Your power is far greater than mine or any earthly justice system. Teach me to trust my battles to Your all-knowing wisdom, righteousness, and power. Amen.

Father, justice in my case would be the end of me. Thank You for not giving me what I deserved. Instead You've taken on Yourself the punishment I deserve and given me what I don't deserve in exchange. Thank You for paying the cost of my sin so that I can walk free—blessed, forgiven, and loved. Your grace is more than I could ever ask for. Amen.

Lord God, I have taken on a just and righteous cause—prayed for it, stood strong for it, demanded it, marched for it, and yet, my so much has gone unchanged. I'm ready to lay it down, let it go, and walk away. But before I do, I put this cry for justice in Your hands. You who are all-powerful. You who are perfectly upright, the Great Judge. I trust You to see this through until justice triumphs. Amen.

Father, I marvel at Your justice and celebrate Your victory! Amen.

What shall we say then? There is no injustice
with God, is there? May it never be!

Dear Jesus, I'm suffering from a great injustice that is impossible to fight on my own. My hands are tied, and my words are meaningless. They can in no way defend me. Your Word says that if You are for me, no one can be against me. I trust You to stand against this injustice on my behalf. I take up my shield of faith and believe You are making things right. Amen.

Lord, I have been treated unjustly. I was polite and civil while others were rude. I was kind and gentle while others were unkind. I was patient while others were angry. At least that's what I tried to do. Truth is, I could use some help turning the other cheek like You did when You were wronged and treated badly. Give me the strength to walk worthy of You by following Your example. Amen.

Father, I'm angry. You know what I've had to endure; how I've been wronged at the hands of another. All legal remedies have failed. You alone continue to promise me justice. I don't know how that will come, but I'm determined to leave my case in Your hands. I continue to trust You to dispense justice. Take away my anger and help me rest in Your assurance that You will one day make all things right. Amen.

KINDNESS

Never let loyalty and kindness leave you!
Tie them around your neck as a reminder.
PROVERBS 3:3 NLT

Dear Lord, every day we must choose to make kindness part of our lives. I choose to be kind to the poor and to those who are alone. I choose to be kind to those living in fear. I choose kindness as my creed; even to those who are unkind, because that's what makes it real. Amen.

Thank You, Father, for the kindness You've shown me. Your kindness softens everything it touches. Amen.

Father, I've known many kindhearted people in my life. Some said kind words and others performed kind acts out of loving hearts. These people have affected me in ways I can't define. Help me be kinder, more careful about the words I speak, quicker to extend a helping hand. Help me honor You and the kind people I've known by becoming a softer, gentler, kinder person to all. Amen.

Father God, kindness doesn't seem to be my first response to people and situations around me—but I want it to be. Help me be more aware of opportunities to be kind, more creative in the ways of kindness, and more committed to pleasing You by making kindness my first response. Amen.

LEADERSHIP

*The most important one of you should be like the
least important, and your leader should be like a servant.*
Luke 22:26 cev

Heavenly Father, in leading others, help me lead by
example in commitment, consistency, and compassion.
Help me be transparent and approachable while I
exercise firm convictions and strength of character.
Keep me humble as I serve others through responsible
leadership. Amen.

People look to me to be a leader, Lord. I don't feel it. Is
that what You want me to be? Amen.

Father, I call You "Lord", and yet I often go my own way,
do my own thing. I find I don't like to "follow the leader"
as much as I did as a child. Cleanse and adjust my heart.
I have been called to follow, and I committed to that
calling when I said I would follow You with all my heart.
Change me, Lord. Amen.

Father, when I was younger, I felt good about being
a leader to Your people. Lately though, it feels like
a burden. So much conflict, heartache, and loss of
relationship with people I care about. I need a change
of attitude, Lord. I need refreshing and a burst of new
passion. I need to be assured that I was called by You.
Search my heart, Lord. Reveal to me any pride or
stubbornness. Cleanse me of any sin. Give me a new love
for the people You've called me to serve. Amen.

LONELINESS

Turn to me and be gracious to me,
for I am lonely and afflicted.
Psalm 25:16 nasb

Heavenly Father, a new season in my life has brought me into a place of loneliness. There are times that I feel alone, even in a room filled with people. You must have felt these same human feelings when You lived here on earth. The Bible says that when Your heart was heavy, You cried out to Your Father. Just as You trusted the nearness of His presence, help me call on You as my friend and companion, remembering that I am never really alone. Amen.

Father, why am I lonely when all around me there is conversation, laughter, music, and motion? With so many people nearby, it would seem that I could never feel alone. But I do, Lord. I fear I've built a wall around myself, closing myself off from others. The problem is that I can't seem to break free of this self-imposed exile. Open my heart, I pray. Open my eyes and ears to those around me. Amen.

Dear Lord, I'm never lonely when I'm alone with You. Amen.

Lord, I feel blessed. There are so many people in my life—friends, family, coworkers, even friends I've yet to meet. But I do see others who are not so blessed. And there are those who I see watching from the sidelines unable to enter in. Help me be a friend to the friendless. Amen.

LOVE FOR FAMILY

It takes wisdom to have a good family,
and it takes understanding to make it strong.
PROVERBS 24:3 NCV

Precious Lord, the love for my family is so great and so deep, it's hard to express in words. We are all different, but the bond we share blesses us with a constant sense of belonging. Let me be a blessing to my family and serve them from the fullness of my heart. At the end of each day, may I be able to say, "I have loved well." Amen.

Father, I'm so thankful for family. Having one another to rely on, sharing the good times and the bad. Thank You for the love we share when we walk and talk, eat, play, and rest together. Thank You for the grace to grow closer still and love each other more. Thank You for the extra ones You add to our families through spiritual birth. It's good to have family, Lord. Amen.

Lord God, thank You for brothers and sisters in the faith. I don't know where I would be without them. They pray for me, support me, and tell me the truth in love. My birth family is badly broken, but my brothers and sisters in the faith have shown me what family should be—what it can be. Thank You for adopting me into Your family, Lord. Amen.

Lord, help me be a beacon of light in my family. Amen.

LOVE FOR GOD

*"YOU SHALL LOVE THE LORD YOUR GOD WITH ALL YOUR HEART,
AND WITH ALL YOUR SOUL, AND WITH ALL YOUR MIND."*
MATTHEW 22:37 NASB

Dear God, when I came to know You personally, I saw what a loving God You are. You show me daily that You care about every detail of my life. You tell me that I am Yours and You call me Your Beloved. Thank You for loving me before I ever loved You. Amen.

I love You, Lord. You are everything to me. Amen.

Lord Jesus, I know You loved me first because I'm sure I wasn't even capable of love until you sought me out and declared Your love for me. I love You because You have been faithful to me. I can trust You to protect me, hear my prayers, walk beside me through my life, and carry me through the roughest spots. Yes, I love You, Lord. Thank You for loving me first. Amen.

Loving Father, I've watched in amazement as people of other religions bow down to their gods. They seem devout, earnest, and resolute, but I've never heard any of them say they loved the gods they were worshipping. Appeasement maybe, gratitude perhaps, devotion possibly—but love? I don't know, and I have no right to judge. I can say though that I truly do love You. Thank You for allowing me to love freely. Amen.

LOVE FOR OTHERS

YOU SHALL LOVE YOUR NEIGHBOR AS YOURSELF.
MATTHEW 22:39 NASB

Dear Lord, I want to make a difference with my life by making a difference in the lives of others. Give me a heart to reach out more and tangibly show the kind of unconditional love to others as You've shown to me. I believe that love is the most powerful force on earth. Help me always remember what I've read in Your Word: "Love never fails." Amen.

Show me someone who is left out and needs a friend, Lord, and I will reach out to be a friend. Amen.

God, make me a person who cares about others. In faith, I will search out opportunities to touch the lonely, feed the hungry, visit those who are in prison, care for the sick and dying. Let my faith be more than wishing everyone health, food, clothes, and a place to live. Let my life show my faith in You by helping those You love whenever I can. Speak and I will obey, Lord. Amen.

Father, it's easy enough to say I love You, but it's *not* so easy to prove my love for You by reaching out to others, especially those who are, in the natural, quite unlovable. Empower me to love as You do—fully and without hesitation. Amen.

LUST/SEXUAL SIN

*Put on the Lord Jesus Christ, and make no
provision for the flesh, to fulfill its lusts.*
ROMANS 13:14 NKJV

Dear Jesus, I've learned through hard lessons that there is no greater need in my life than my need for You. Let the greatest desires of my heart be for You rather than selfish interests and possessions. You, always, first, and only. Amen.

Father, can You show me the difference between love and lust? It's hard to tell them apart these days. Amen.

God, make me diligent to protect my heart from lust— from wanting what is not mine, from the far-reaching struggle to get more, to have pleasures and possessions that are not good or pure or holy. Let me begin by cleaning out my heart. Help me get rid of the envy and lustful thoughts that make me vulnerable. Forgive and cleanse me and make me fully committed to You. Amen.

Dear Father, I thought lust was a man's problem and that it had to do with sex. I finally looked it up, and guess what? Lust is actually an overwhelming desire for something I don't have. It isn't fixated on a person like with envy but on a possession, a thing. Well…about that handbag I bought even though I knew we couldn't afford it. I see now that was wrong, that was lust. Help me keep my desires under control, Lord, and completely surrendered to You. Amen.

*In sexual sin we violate the sacredness of our
own bodies, these bodies that were made for
God-given and God-modeled love.*
1 CORINTHIANS 6:18 MSG

Heavenly Father, recent news of a dear friend caught
in sexual sin has devastated me. While I don't condone
his behavior, I realize I'm not his judge. I want to help,
but the best way I know to do that is to pray. Take the
blinders from his eyes and reveal to him the destructive
nature of his actions. Bring conviction and repentance as
You draw him back to Your heart. Amen.

Father, I've failed—though failed seems a trivial way
to describe it. What I've done has such far-reaching
consequences. It seems like too much to ask You to
forgive, though I know in my head that Your sacrifice
was great enough to cover *all* sin. I ask You to cleanse me,
Lord, and set my feet again on the path of righteousness.
I place all my hope in Your unconditional love and
forgiveness. Amen.

Lord God, I used to stand in awe of Your holiness, but
now I fear it. Knowing there will be a reckoning for my
sin causes dread to rise up in my throat. I'm truly sorry
for my sin, Lord, but I also know I'm a slave to it. Have
mercy on me, Lord. Reach out to those I've harmed and
heal them. I surrender myself to You for correction and
cleansing. Amen.

MARRIAGE

*It's good for a man to have a wife,
and for a woman to have a husband.*
1 CORINTHIANS 7:2 MSG

Dear Lord, what a gift You gave me when You blessed me with a partner, soulmate, and companion to share my journey through life. When committed love between two people is centered in You, it becomes a holy joy beyond what earthly words can describe. Thank You for giving me someone to love. Amen.

Oh Lord, I'm not sure I'm ready to be married. Teach me and then lead me to the person You have chosen for me. Amen.

Lord, I'm concerned that marriage seems to be almost obsolete these days. So many feel it's just a formality or something they will get around to at some point. They overlook the importance of the commitment and underestimate the effect that lack of commitment will have on their homes and families. I pray that the sanctity of marriage would once again reign in our society. Amen.

Father, I've always thought I would meet the one—the person You prepared for me. But I'm still waiting. Truth is I do pretty well on my own. Just the same, my heart aches with longing for someone to love, someone to give myself to, someone to raise children with. I ask You, Lord, to send that special person across my path. And if that is not Your plan for me, settle my heart and show me how to be content. Amen.

MISSIONS

*"Go into the world. Go everywhere and announce
the Message of God's good news to one and all."*
MARK 16:16 MSG

Dear Jesus, help those who risk all and sacrifice their comfort and security for the sake of sharing the Gospel. Protect them, guide them, and let them feel Your presence as You keep them safely in Your care. Prepare the hearts of all they minister to, and help them receive what is poured out through Your Ambassadors of Love. Amen.

Father, when I was a child I dreamed of becoming a missionary. I read every missionary story I could find and relished the visits of missionary speakers at church. I found I had a heart for sharing the Gospel. I was disappointed when my life didn't go in that direction. But now I realize that my mission field has been in my own family, among my acquaintances, and in my community. I praise You for Your perfect plan. Thank You for making my childhood dream come true. Amen.

Lord, I pray for those who are in danger around the world as they deliver the precious message of Your love and sacrifice to all men and women everywhere. I pray You would provide for them, encourage them, strengthen them, and inspire them as they continue on through difficult circumstances. Also, Lord, I pray that You would show me how to help those who are taking Your message to the world. Amen.

MERCY

"Blessed are the merciful,
for they will be shown mercy."
MATTHEW 5:7 NIV

Heavenly Father, I've come to realize that there are both strengths and weaknesses when exercising the gift of mercy. Give me insight and wisdom concerning how to set boundaries. Protect me from becoming a compassionate enabler, and help me guide others to the greatest source of mercy—You. Amen.

Today I saw a homeless man, Lord. He didn't ask for anything and I didn't give him anything. Should I have shown mercy to him? Amen.

Lord, Your mercy is everlasting and yet new every day. You are merciful to us in ways we cannot expect or explain. Teach us to show mercy like You do because we know Your definition is not always the same as ours. We see like someone walking in the dark—we feel our way along. Help us, Father. Thank You that Your mercy shines brightest in our lives when we definitely don't deserve it. Amen.

Lord God, thank You for reaching down and having mercy on me. I was completely lost, but You showed me the way. I was in great distress, but You held my hand and comforted me. I was blind to the things that really matter, but You cleared up my eyesight. Thank You, Lord. Amen.

MINISTRY

The real *believers are the ones the Spirit of God leads to work away at this ministry, filling the air with Christ's praise as we do it.*
PHILIPPIANS 3:3 MSG

Dear God, I don't take ministry and serving others lightly. Let all I do flow out of a heart that is filled with Your love. Pour into me what You can trust me to pour out to others. Help me remember that ministry is not what I do, but what and who I am in You. Amen.

Thank You, Lord, for my Sunday school teacher. Every week she teaches me about You. Amen.

Father, I want to work and serve You in some way, and I know You are the one who gave me that desire. Guard my thoughts and actions so that I might minister to others with a pure heart and clean hands. Give me wisdom so that I can help Your children find answers to their questions and solutions for their problems. Help me find my workplace in Your Kingdom of Light. Amen.

Lord, I think back to all the godly people I have encountered, those who ministered to me when I so desperately needed it. I know You prepared them and planned for our paths to cross. Thank You for hearing my pleas for help and sending Your precious ones to minister to me. Amen.

MODESTY

I also want the women to be modest and
sensible about their clothes and to dress properly.
1 TIMOTHY 2:9 GNT

Dear Jesus, as our culture and society becomes more
liberal in the media, in fashion, and in literature, it's easy
to become complacent about what is considered decent
and right in Your eyes. Compromise can be deceiving
and downright dangerous. Help me be an advocate
for living and representing the kind of modesty that is
pleasing to You. Amen.

Lord, I need to know how to deal with all the peer
pressure I get when it comes to clothes. Give me courage,
I pray. Amen.

God, it's hard these days to escape the constant barrage
of skintight and low-cut clothing. I don't want to place
myself or anyone else under the bondage of abandoning
fashion and obsessing over keeping every inch of skin
covered. I only pray that You will help me maintain
modesty and teach modesty to my children so we will all
be pleasing to You. Amen.

Father God, help me strive to please You and not make a
spectacle of myself in the way I dress, my body language,
my attitude, my words, or my actions. I pray that I would
do nothing to lessen the light of Your presence from
shining forth to others. Amen.

MONEY

The love of money is a root of all kinds of evil.
Some people, eager for money, have wandered from
the faith and pierced themselves with many griefs.
1 Timothy 6:10 niv

Dear Lord, help me keep a balanced perspective about money, the need for it and the use of it. Help me remember that money is a tool to help me live life and provide for my needs. Help me avoid squandering it or make it an idol, and instead use it wisely, respecting the power of what it represents. Amen.

Father, my mother once told me she prayed that she would never be rich because all that money might lead her to believe she no longer needed You to meet her needs. She also prayed that she would not be poor. That, she believed, might cause her to steal in order to eat. Of course, these were her personal thoughts only, but her solution was interesting. She prayed instead, that You would give her just enough to meet her needs. Thank you for providing just what I need as well. And if I find myself with more or less, thank You for sending the grace to deal with it. Amen.

Father, it takes money to survive in this world and so many have too little. I pray that every dollar that comes into my hands will be a way to meet my basic needs and those of others. Give me eyes that recognize those who are truly in need and a heart to be Your channel of blessing. Amen.

MOTIVES

All a person's ways seem pure to them,
but motives are weighed by the Lord.
PROVERBS 16:2 NIV

Precious Jesus, I want everything I do to be done with
right motives. Filter my motives through a heart that is
open to hear Your correction and Your wisdom. As my
physical heart needs a filter for life-giving blood to flow
from it, let my spiritual heart be a filter for all of the
choices I make. Amen.

Father, I pray for pure motives so that all I do will
be pleasing in Your eyes. Knock on the door of my
conscience when I entertain greedy thoughts, selfish
thoughts, thoughts of envy and jealousy. I want so
much to be like You, but all too easily, my humanness
threatens to rob me of my inner truth. Light my path,
Lord. Examine my inner thoughts and wash them
clean. Amen.

Lord God, You have placed me in a position of authority.
I pray that You will give me discernment. Help me see
when there are hidden motives in those who serve under
me. Show me my own inner motives as well, Lord. I want
to be worthy of this responsibility You've given me. Amen.

Lord God, help me show my children that right things
must be done for the right reasons. Amen.

NEW BABY/PARENTHOOD

*God's ways are as mysterious as the pathway of the wind and
as the manner in which a human spirit is infused into the
little body of a baby while it is yet in its mother's womb.*
ECCLESIASTES 11:5 TLB

Dear God, the new baby that is now a part of my life has
already changed me, filled my heart with an abundance
of love, and caused me to pause and praise You. Thank
You for the joy this small child brings to so many. Amen.

God, our new little one is here. We weren't expecting
this to happen so quickly, but here she is. Truthfully, I
feel somewhat unprepared. There is still so much we
don't know. Help us do a good job raising this little one,
seeking Your guidance in all things. Amen.

Father God, we weren't expecting this baby. We had our
lives pretty well planned out. We aren't young parents,
so this will be a real challenge. But, I'm sitting here with
this little one in my arms, and my heart is exploding
with happiness. Thank You for overruling our plans and
replacing them with Your own. Amen.

Lord, these two little darlings needed us as much as we
needed them. Our meeting seems so unlikely, but we
have to smile when we think about how You brought
us together—two parentless children and two childless
parents. Thanks. Amen.

He will make peace between parents and their
children and will bring those who are not obeying
God back to the right way of thinking.
LUKE 1:17 NCV

Dear Lord, the tremendous challenges and responsibilities of parenting are daunting at best; but the honor and opportunity to help shape and prepare a child for life is truly a gift of wonder and grace. I thank You for the gift and the everyday blessings that come with parenthood. Amen.

Father, raising these children is a tough job. But I find great joy and fulfillment in parenthood—no matter what problems and troubles I face with my kids, no matter what pain they have given me. I love them so much. I'm so glad You gave them to me. I pray that I'll be equal to the job You've entrusted to me. Amen.

No kidding, Lord, I thought I might not make it through today. Some days my three children seem like thirty-three. I ask for grace to deal with the unexpected and patience to manage drama and hormones. I could also use a hand with my organizational skills. Thanks for the privilege of raising a family, Lord. Even on the worst of days, I know what a blessed woman I am. Amen.

I'm going to need some help communicating with my kids, Lord. Sometimes I think they must be speaking a foreign language. Amen.

NEW BEGINNINGS

What we see is that anyone united with the Messiah gets a fresh start, is created new. The old life is gone; a new life burgeons!
2 CORINTHIANS 5:17 MSG

Heavenly Father, where would I be without the mercy You extend to me each day? You bring with every rising sun new beginnings. You give me a clean slate. You paint a new picture across the canvas of my life—a picture of Your blessings as they unfold. Teach me, even when it's hard to let go of my safe places, to trust the new beginnings You bring into my life. Amen.

Father, this new endeavor I'm facing is daunting—and very exciting. Help me keep my head on straight, making wise decisions and listening for Your voice. I really do want to make the best of this opportunity. Thank You for going along with me, showing me the way one day at a time. Amen.

Lord, You've given me a brand new life. I'm worried though because I'm pretty sure I'm the same old person. Nothing will change unless I change, and I can't change on my own. Go to work on me, Lord. Dig down deep and deal with all those things that got me in trouble before so that I can handle them differently this time. Thank You for this chance to start over. I'm looking to You this time to help me make a go of it. Amen.

OBEDIENCE

Those who obey the LORD are daily in his care,
and what he has given them will be theirs forever.
PSALM 37:18 CEV

Dear God, You teach in Your Word that obedience is better than sacrifice. So often what You speak to my spirit seems too hard to do. The person You instruct me to go to and pray with; the phone call of apology I need to make; the money You ask me to give are all obedience issues beyond my comfort zone. God, help me heed Your instructions and walk them out in obedience. Amen.

Father, I know a good father demands obedience not of other peoples' children but of his own. I love being Yours, even though You reprimand me when I do something wrong. For me, that's proof that You love me and care what happens in my life. You care about my situation, my relationships, and my future. Thanks for loving me. Amen.

Lord, I want to quickly obey, but honestly, sometimes I can't tell what You want me to do. Show me how to please You, Father, with my obedience. Amen.

Father, I don't want to just obey, I want to obey with all my heart, with a mind fully persuaded that Your ways are best. Give me the confidence I need to do what You say, when You say it, and to trust that I can discern Your voice and understand what You want from me. Amen.

OPPRESSION

I sing praises to you, LORD. You rescue the oppressed.
JEREMIAH 20:13 CEV

Dear God, the oppression I'm experiencing is taking a toll on me spiritually, mentally, emotionally, and physically. It's worn me down and left me feeling too weak to fight against it. Help me rise up in the authority You've given me to take a stand against the powers and principalities of darkness. Renew the overcomer in me. Help me banish and conquer the oppression and the oppressor. Amen.

Lord, watching the news and reading the papers can be frightening. There is so much grief and hurt and prejudice and hate in the world. Let me see the truth and know the peace You give that passes understanding. Lift the oppression that threatens to steal my joy and make me forget how greatly I'm blessed. Amen.

Father, thank You for allowing me to live in a country where I'm free, where my words and actions are not prescribed and dictated. Thank You for all those who died ensuring that freedom. I pray for those who live under oppressive governments around the world. Amen.

No outward force can strip me of my relationship with You, Lord. For that, I praise You with my whole heart. Amen.

PAST

*Do not hold past sins against us; let Your compassion
come to us quickly, for we have become weak.*
PSALM 79:8 HCSB

Heavenly Father, the enemy loves to taunt me with
memories and guilt from my past. Your Word says my
past sins have been thrown into the sea of forgetfulness.
You never hold my past against me. Help me close my
heart and mind to the lies of the enemy. Thank You that
I can walk free from my past today because You loved me
and paid the price for my sins. Amen.

Thank You, Lord, for a future full of hope and promise—
my past remembered no more. Amen.

God, I'm sure You have forgiven me. Nevertheless, a
parade of sins, mistakes, failures, and pains rush after
me—ghosts of my past. Help me keep my mind stayed
on the future. Teach me to move forward without
looking left or right and certainly not over my shoulder!
Give me courage to leave the past and look to tomorrow
with joy. Amen.

Father, I know my past is forgiven and behind me. Help
me remember only the lessons learned so that I will not
stumble over the same old sins I was vulnerable to before.
Safeguard my freedom with healthy reminders to keep
me on the straight path. Amen.

PATIENCE

*May you be prepared to endure
everything with patience.*
COLOSSIANS 1:11 NRSV

Dear Jesus, You know that patience doesn't come easy for me. You've seen me try to fix situations or hurry along Your plans instead of waiting for Your divine timing. Teach me to be content in Your waiting room, remembering that You make all things beautiful in Your time. Amen.

Lord, I ask for a quiet heart as I wait for Your promises, trusting that Your timing is always best. Help me also develop a habit of patience with all those around me just as You have been so patient with me. Amen.

I want patience, Lord, but waiting leaves me frustrated. I guess that's the problem right there! Thank You for being so patient with me. Amen.

Father, I've noticed that my children don't know how to wait. They were born into a world of instant everything. But learning patience is the difference between waiting for the best and settling for something less. I want my children to learn to wait before You, to listen for Your voice. Show me ways to introduce the joy of waiting into my children's consciousness and teach them its merits. Amen.

PERSECUTION

*"In the world you face persecution.
But take courage; I have conquered the world!"*
JOHN 16:33 NRSV

Dear Lord, I don't understand why believing in You sometimes brings persecution. Your Word clearly confirms we will endure persecution, but sometimes it's hard for my faith to rise above and overcome the things that hurt my heart. I remember the persecutions You suffered for my sake. Help me remember that mine are light in comparison, and Your eternal grace is greater than any of my temporary sufferings. Amen.

Lord Jesus, persecution hasn't touched my life—at least not directly. I've never been mistreated because of my faith or beliefs. For this I'm thankful. But I'm aware that across the world, scores of people are targeted for abuse and even death because they dare to stand for what is right. I commit to support them with my prayers. I pray that You would comfort, strengthen, and protect them. Amen.

Thank You, Lord, for helping me stand up and defend my commitment to You whenever and wherever it is challenged. Amen.

I pray, Father, for those who are persecuted because of the color of their skin or the culture they were born into. I want to feel the anger You must feel when any part of Your beautiful and unique creation is denigrated. I ask You to take my anger and use it in positive ways. Amen.

PERSEVERANCE

May the Lord direct your hearts into
God's love and Christ's perseverance.
2 Thessalonians 3:5 niv

Precious Lord, each day You help me run my race and keep me moving forward. Even when I think I can't take one more step of faith or endure one more challenging circumstance, You infuse me with strength that is not my own. You help me keep believing and moving forward. Thank You for the spirit of perseverance You've instilled in me. Use it to sustain me through every challenge. Amen.

Lord, so many times I want to give up. I wonder if what I'm doing is worthwhile or am I just wasting my time. Help me see beyond my now and into the future. Give me a glimpse of how my life and work will benefit others, and Lord, let this be the impetus for me to keep on keeping on. Amen.

Lord, You encountered impossible obstacles but You kept on doing Your Father's will. If You had given up, there would have been no hope for me. Now You are asking me to persevere just a little, stay in place until the work is done, and not quit before my efforts pay off. Strengthen me, Lord, and let me feel Your presence with me until victory arrives. Amen.

Help me, Lord, to stick with the little tasks You give me so that I will be able to stick with the big tasks that will one day come. Amen.

PEACE

Look at those who are honest and good,
for a wonderful future awaits those who love peace.
PSALM 37:37 NLT

Dear God, there is nothing in my walk with You that compares to Your peace. The kind that surpasses my human understanding. The kind that calms the storms of my anxious soul. The peace that whispers to simply "be still and know." Thank You for being my peace speaker and my peacekeeper. Amen.

Father, I have a home, health, and friends, but somehow peace eludes me. I know that I should be able to know Your marvelous peace wherever I am—even if I were locked away in a prison cell. Help me keep my mind and heart stayed on You and Your hand in my life. Pour peace over me like melted gold when I trust in You. Amen.

Father, our peace has been shattered by war. Everywhere I look I see destruction and brokenness. I pray that peace would return to my homeland. I ask that peace would be restored before even more damage can be done. Until then, keep all of us safe. Amen.

Father, I ask for a few minutes of peace from the turmoil of this day. As I close my eyes, I pray that Your peace will wash over me like an ocean wave. Amen.

POVERTY

Speak up for the poor and helpless,
and see that they get justice.
PROVERBS 31:9 NLT

Dear heavenly Father, so many are living their lives
with barely enough resources to survive. The desire of
my heart is to help meet the needs of those in poverty
whenever and however I am able. Despite my modest
means, I want to share whatever blessings I've been
given. Give me a heart of compassion to help alleviate
the suffering that poverty brings. Amen.

Lord, I see it all around me, in third-world countries, on
television, in both cities and rural places—poverty, like a
grim reaper. I feel compassion for the poor, but I want to
do something about it. Give me work and opportunity,
Lord, so that I can fight poverty at least in the life of one
other person. Help me share my resources in a way that
is pleasing to You. Amen.

Lord, here I am again. As always we need provision for
the rent and utilities. We were able to get some food
at the food bank, but I have nothing to cover the rest.
You've always supplied what we need one way or another.
Help me remember that we are rich because You are our
provider. Amen.

Heavenly Father, thank You for this food You've
provided. You never let us down. Amen.

PRAISE

I will praise thee, O Lord, with my whole heart;
I will shew forth all thy marvellous works.
PSALM 9:1 KJV

Dear Lord, before there are answers to my prayers, give me a heart to praise You. Let my praise be the voice of faith that sings hope to my spirit and my thankfulness to Your heart. Inhabit my praise and let me feel Your presence overtake every doubt or fear that clouds my vision. Lord, I can never praise or thank You enough for all You've done for me. Amen.

Father, I want to praise You because of the wondrous creation You have given us. You could have made us and everything around us the same—flowers all the same color, trees with only one type of leaf, vegetables all long and thin, animals all the same shape and size, and the whole year without seasonal changes. Instead, You made all things wonderful, delightful, colorful, and splendid. I praise You, my wonderful creator God. Amen.

I owe You a debt of praise, Lord, but my heart refuses to give voice to it. It feels dark and heavy within me. Nevertheless, I will instruct my lips to praise You and pray that my heart will follow. You deserve so much more than my broken emotions. Please accept my praise despite that which is obviously lacking. Amen.

With my whole heart, Lord God, I sing Your praises for all to hear. I'm so pleased to be Your child. Amen.

PRIDE/VANITY

All that is in the world, the lust of the flesh, and the lust of the eyes, and the pride of life, is not of the Father, but is of the world.
1 JOHN 2:16 KJV

Dear God, I didn't mean to let pride slip into a situation that has hurt me and caused hurt to others. Forgive me for having a prideful attitude and thinking I could handle things without going to You first. Humble my heart so that I will always depend on You as my counselor, my all-knowing source, and my wise Father. Amen.

Lord, cure me of my pride. When someone offers help, I feel myself resist. When someone seems to look down on me, I bristle. When I hear a whisper or laugh, I imagine someone is judging me. Such nonsense, Lord. Help me conquer my prideful heart so that I can follow You in humility and a gentle spirit. Amen.

I've had several significant falls, Lord, and still I haven't learned that pride is not my friend. It brings me down every time and spoils the good I might have done. Amen.

I see it even at church, Lord—so many egos, so much pride, those who think they are better than everyone else. Cleanse Your church of this insidious black mold. As long as it persists, our efforts to carry out Your mission will be polluted and ineffective. Start the cleansing with me, Lord. Amen.

Turn away mine eyes from beholding vanity;
and quicken thou me in thy way.
PSALM 119:37 KJV

Precious Lord, society seems to be obsessed with vanity. I see the evidence on magazine covers, social media, and television. Vanity's voice is outward, selfish, prideful, and self-absorbed. As one who serves and follows You, help me keep humility as a guard for my inner heart against becoming involved in vanity's trappings. Amen.

Some plans look good on the surface, Lord, but down at the core they are rotten, filled with vanity and pride. These efforts waste precious time and amount to nothing in the end. Help us see them for what they are and reject them as distractions, designed to keep us from the good work of the Kingdom. Amen.

Hold a mirror to my heart, Lord. Let me see what is really there so I can surrender myself to Your cleansing down deep in my core. I desire to be altogether pleasing to You. Amen.

Lord, I feel like I'm fat and ugly. Mom and Dad say that's a lie that I have decided to believe. They say You created me, and I'm beautiful and unique. That sure isn't what I hear at school. I want to believe that You really do think I'm beautiful. Help me throw away the lies and find out who I really am. Amen.

PURITY

Set an example for the believers in speech,
in conduct, in love, in faith and in purity.
1 TIMOTHY 4:12 NIV

Dear Lord, so many attitudes and grievances muddy the water of my soul. Take away the dross and clutter that separate me from the purity of Your Spirit. Cleanse my thoughts and create a new heart in me—one that is more like You. Prepare me for the holiness of Your presence. Amen.

Lord, create a clean heart in me. Rid me of any impure thoughts or deeds. Help me be above reproach in my daily living. Teach me to turn away from anything that would stain and pollute my heart or my testimony. Protect and teach my inner man to be a person of integrity. Amen.

Father, the sin nature inside me will always leave me short of purity. That's why I thank You for the pure and gentle Jesus who dwells within, lending His spotless presence to all I am and all I do. Amen.

I'm pretty inexperienced in the affairs of this world, Lord. Stay near and help me keep my hands clean and my heart acceptable to You. When I mess up, I receive the gift of Your forgiveness to make me pure again. Amen.

RECOGNITION

*Do not withhold good from those to whom
it is due, when it is in your power to act.*
PROVERBS 3:27 NIV

Dear God, it can be a great stumbling block to constantly need a pat on the back or recognition for the things we do. Help me do what I do for Your glory and not for anyone's applause. Help me remember that Yours is the only applause I desire or need. Amen.

Lord Jesus, my mom and dad work so hard to take care of all of us. Please bless my mom and dad in a special way. Amen.

Lord, I see those individuals who are working for You and for the good of others. Show me ways that I can give them recognition for their efforts that bless us all. It's difficult to serve when you feel no one notices what you're doing. Let me be among those who speak up and blesses. Amen.

Father, it seems like all anyone cares about at work is who gets the credit. There is so much jockeying for position that it makes my head spin. I need some kind of strategy to keep me from getting caught up in the middle of it all. When Your disciples kept asking who is the greatest, You set them straight with a few timely words. Show me how to still the overactive egos in my world. Amen.

RECONCILIATION

*All things are of God, who has reconciled us to Himself through
Jesus Christ, and has given us the ministry of reconciliation.*
2 CORINTHIANS 5:18 NKJV

Dear Lord, my heart is shattered over a broken friendship. Knowing Your love for unity and wholeness, I ask
You to help me take the first step toward reconciliation.
Let me speak healing words and be the first to apologize,
regardless of fault. Help me remember that being right is
not worth the pain of being without my friend. Amen.

Father, my family desperately needs Your help. I can't
remember now where it started, but one disagreement
turned into more. Soon it became a swirling whirlpool
of hurt and misunderstanding. I ask that You would put
out the raging fires of anger and resentment and help us
broker a plan for peace that includes apologies spoken,
forgiveness given, and relationships healed. Thank You
even now for a new era of love and understanding in our
family. Amen.

Father God, thank You for opening the way for me to have
a relationship with You. Without Jesus and His sacrifice,
my sin would always separate us. Instead, I've been granted
the gift of reconciliation with You. My heart is constantly
singing a song of thanksgiving. Amen.

Lord, my father was never in my life but now he's here
asking for a chance to know me. Give me the grace I
need to open my heart. Amen.

REGRET

*The sadness that is used by God brings a change of heart
that leads to salvation—and there is no regret in that!*

2 Corinthians 7:10 GNT

Dear Jesus, regret feels so much like guilt at times. I
replay things in my mind, thinking of all the ways I
could have done things differently. I waste a lot of time
agonizing over the "if's" and "why's" of things I've done
and said. Help me release my regrets and the weight of
guilt I've carried. I choose to live in this moment and
move forward by Your grace. Amen.

Father, I've reached out for Your forgiveness, but I can't
seem to let go of the regret I feel for my actions. I feel
like to do so would be saying the things I did and the
people I hurt were of no importance. Help me focus on
the blood of Jesus that covers my past sins and the gentle
comfort of the Holy Spirit poured out on those who
suffered at my hand. Thank You, Lord, for helping me
realize my freedom one step at a time. Amen.

I regret so many things I've done in my past, but I will
never regret my decision to invite You into my life. Thank
You for the joy of knowing You. Amen.

Lord, help me take my regrets and transform them
into learning experiences that will help me make good
choices in the future. Amen.

RELATIONSHIPS

All this comes from the God who settled the relationship
between us and him, and then called us to settle
our relationships with each other.
2 CORINTHIANS 5:18 MSG

Heavenly Father, as time passes, my love and gratitude grow stronger for my family and friends. Thank You for allowing these special people to share my life's journey. Help me be a heart-tender to them as we share tears and joy, triumphs and struggles. Keep them safe, and bless them with good health and well-being. Help me never take relationships for granted, but let me honor them always with my time and devotion. Amen.

Lord Jesus, a lot of my relationships have been lost through my own carelessness. I've neglected them until they withered away. I've lost more than I care to acknowledge. Help me as I strive to be a friend to those You send my way—a good and caring friend. Amen.

Holy Father, thank You for the people You've placed in my life. I'm thankful for all of them, even those who aren't easy to be around and make me want to run and hide. Those seem to be the ones who help me see the truth about myself. Thank You also for those who are a constant encouragement and whose love for me fills my heart each day. Amen.

Thank You, Lord, for being the best friend I could ever have. Amen.

RENEWAL

Restore unto me the joy of thy salvation;
and uphold me with thy free spirit.
PSALM 51:12 KJV

Dear God, it's impossible to keep up a busy daily schedule, tasks, and responsibilities without an occasional time-out. It's hard for me to slow down and just "be" rather than always doing. Without renewal and rest, I know I'm going to burn out. I can't pour out to others from an empty vessel. Refresh my weary soul and body as I stop, rest, and wait for You to renew and fill me once again. Amen.

Father, I see it now. My prayers have grown routine and impersonal. My worship is cold and stale. I confess my lack of sincerity, Lord, my careless neglect of the most important relationship in my life. Light my candle again, I pray. Renew my heart through Your Word, music, and fellowship. Restore to me the joy of my salvation. Thank You, Father. Amen.

Lord, thank You for recognizing my condition and giving me a much-needed infusion of Your love and peace. You always seem to know when I'm becoming passive and mediocre in my faith, when I need a new touch, a new burst of energy, a new vision. Thanks for insisting that I always give You my best. Amen.

New, Lord—I feel so new and clean and excited about the future. Thank You, Lord. Amen.

REPENTANCE

I restore the crushed spirit of the humble and
revive the courage of those with repentant hearts.
ISAIAH 57:15 NLT

Dear Jesus, please do not let my mind and heart become dull to my need for repentance. Quicken my spirit when I've made a mistake and need to ask to be forgiven. You forgave me when I committed my life to You, but we both know I will never be perfect even as I strive to be righteous. Give me a ready, repentant, and steadfast heart before You in my daily walk. Amen.

Father, help me remember all the times that You have forgiven me. My heart is prideful, and I hold back from forgiving others, even though I know that it's what You want. Give me more compassion and a merciful spirit so that I will be able to forgive those who sin against me. Let me show Your good heart to others. Amen.

Forgive me, Lord. Only You can make me clean and whole. Amen.

Lord God, I've moved away from You. It was slight, almost imperceptible, especially at first. I didn't even notice until I was nearly out of shouting distance. I thought I would never be in this place, but here I am. Forgive me, Lord. I offer my crime to You with a repentant heart. Draw me back to Your side and stop me in my tracks if I ever drift away again. Amen.

REST

Yes, my soul, find rest in God;
my hope comes from him.
PSALM 62:5 NIV

Dear Lord, when You were here on this earth, You took time away from the crowds to be alone and rest. Remind me that I also need to find a quiet place to recover. Amen.

Lord, like a child exhausted after a long day, I need to be carried in the strong arms of my father. I am worn and weary and need to rest and regain my resolve to go on in this earthly journey. Thank You that I can depend on You and rest safely in Your care. Forgive me when I struggle on in my own waning strength thinking I can make it. Carry me, I pray. Amen.

O Lord, I love my parents so much, but taking care of them is about to break me. I'm desperate for rest, a little sleep, some time for myself. I never imagined I would be in this situation. I thought these years would be filled with travel and hobbies and volunteer work. Instead, I dread getting up in the morning and fall into bed at night. I need relief, Lord. My strength is failing. Send help I pray, and help me find some physical and mental rest. Amen.

Thank You, Lord, for spiritual rest—knowing I don't need to work to earn Your love. You give it freely. Amen.

RETIREMENT

"I'll say to myself, Self, you've done well! You've got it made and can now retire. Take it easy and have the time of your life!"
LUKE 12:19 MSG

Lord, retirement has come too soon for me. I can't help feeling that I have been relegated to the sidelines—that I've lost my usefulness. Help me, Lord, to look through the files of my life's work and see what experience I have gained and what wisdom can be gleaned. Then help me find people who need those scraps of wisdom and know-how. Let me become useful again. Amen.

Dear God, it's challenging to exchange an entire mindset and routine for a life of retirement. As that time approaches, prepare me for the emotional changes I know will come. Ignite my sense of purpose to embrace this new chapter in my life. Help me live each day, knowing my latter years will be greater and more fulfilling than my former years. Amen.

Okay, Lord, now what? I'm feeling pretty useless and unproductive these days. Show me what I'm supposed to be doing during this retirement period of my life. Amen.

Father, I've spent my life so far taking care of responsibilities and doing what is expected of me. Now it's my turn. Refire me, Lord. I'm excited about having time to devote to Kingdom work. Lead the way and I will follow, Lord. I can hardly wait to get started. Amen.

RIGHTEOUSNESS

*Whoever pursues righteousness and unfailing
love will find life, righteousness, and honor.*
PROVERBS 21:21 NLT

Heavenly Father, my heart's desire is to live righteously
before You and others. In our current culture, it's easy
to become complacent and compromising in our views.
Sometimes I see too much and overlook too much.
Help me grow in righteousness through my choices and
know when to stand up for what is right. Guard my
spirit and help me turn away from anything that is not
from You. Amen.

Lord, the pastor talked about righteousness this morning, but it still seems like such a big word, practically
unobtainable. Show me how to break it down into
smaller pieces with clear-cut boundaries. In each situation I encounter today, show me how to do what is right
in Your sight. Amen.

Thank You, Lord, for covering me with the righteousness
of Jesus. I could never measure up on my own. Amen.

Lord, You are righteous. You are sinless. How can I ever
attain that state? Your promise is what I cling to—that
You have forgiven me and by Your own blood, made me
righteous. You took away my clothing, which was stained
with my sins and gave me a clean and holy garment to
wear. This is the hope I have for salvation. Thank You for
this priceless gift. Amen.

REVIVAL

Won't you revive us again, so your people can rejoice in you?
PSALM 85:6 NLT

Dear Jesus, I've heard for many years that revival is coming, but I've just now realized that revival must begin in my heart. How can I pray for others to do what I have not done? Set me on fire, Lord. Revive my heart and soul. Then I will be an inspiration and hope to others that they too can have a new fire of passion for You and Your Kingdom. Amen.

Father, thank You for Your Holy Spirit. When I feel my passion for spiritual things growing dimmer, I invite You to come and rekindle the flame. Soon I feel more excited than ever to pursue eternal objectives. Amen.

O Lord, send Your Holy Spirit to touch hearts and revive Your people. Amen.

Father, give us a revival in our country. Bring our hearts back to You. Let this revival begin in my life with repentance and a clean heart, with sincere prayer and a spirit of gratitude. I want to be close to You, feel Your hand in mine. Then I'll be ready to take hands with my brothers and sisters spreading that contagious laugh of joy Your presence always brings. Amen.

ROMANTIC LOVE

You have captured my heart.
Song of Solomon 4:9 NLT

Dear God, thank You for the beauty and gift of romance. It's mysterious and sacred. Help me never lose my awe and wonder of love and what it means to share it with someone. Keep romance vibrant enough in my heart to make my mate feel special, honored, and adored. Amen.

Father, I was certain he was the one. My heart would actually sing when he was around. Now I'm seeing some things that aren't so enchanting. I long for true love—but I must invest that love in someone who loves You as much as I do. Give me a glimpse of the real person inside and guide me carefully through the waves of emotion to the right one before I give my heart away. Amen.

O Lord Jesus, help my parents like my boyfriend, and if they don't, help me remember that my parents only want Your best for me. Amen.

Father, when Valentine's Day rolls around, I often feel disappointed and isolated, even though I know You are the love of my life. Help those who feel like love has missed them. Help them see that You love them and You long to be loved by them in return. How precious it is to know that we are cherished by You—that You call us Your bride. Amen.

SACRIFICE

*The sacrifices of God are a broken spirit: a broken
and a contrite heart, O God, thou wilt not despise.*
PSALM 51:17 KJV

Heavenly Father, I trust that You know what's best for
me, but sometimes sacrifice is the hardest part of loving
and serving You. Bring acceptance to my heart as I learn
to let go and surrender all to You. When I'm asked to
give up something or someone, help me remember how
much You've sacrificed for me. Amen.

Lord God, each day I make sacrifices for my children
and my spouse. I always put them first, but sometimes
I become resentful because those sacrifices aren't
acknowledged. Of course, I quickly regret those feelings
when I remember how much You sacrificed for me.
Remind me that when we put others first, we are
demonstrating the magnitude of our love for them—and
for You. Amen.

My body is wracked with pain, Lord. And yet, I choose
to offer You my praise—a sacrifice of praise. Amen.

Lord, You loved us and gave Your very life for us. How
can we conceive of such love, so far beyond our human
capacity? You said that for a good man some would even
dare to die, but while we were sinners You died for us.
You sacrificed everything. You gave up Your place in
glory; You faced slander and abuse and death. My thanks
seems so inadequate. Amen.

SALVATION

When he was made perfect, he became the source
of eternal salvation for all those who obey him.
HEBREWS 5:9 GNT

Dear Jesus, how do I thank You for loving me enough to die for me? You exchanged Your life for mine, and You did it all to set me free and give me the gift of eternal life. Even when life is difficult, my heart is filled with joy because You live in me. Help me share the great joy of salvation with others who need to know the kind of grace and unconditional love You've provided for them. Amen.

You, Lord, and You alone have saved me from myself, my sin, and given me a song to sing. Amen.

Father, I tried to save myself by being as good as I could possibly be, but it was never enough. I kept making mistakes—small mistakes but mistakes just the same. Despite my best efforts, I missed the mark. Finally, I acknowledged my need for a Savior and You were there. You welcomed me and washed me clean. Thanks, Lord. I'm grateful every day. Amen.

Lord, I thank You for the salvation You have freely given me. I am set free by the fact that I am completely forgiven and my sins are as far from me as the east is from the west. Thank You for presenting me with such a merciful and undeserved gift. Amen.

SELF-DISCIPLINE

No discipline seems enjoyable at the time, but painful.
Later on, however, it yields the fruit of peace and
righteousness to those who have been trained by it.
HEBREWS 12:11 HCSB

Dear God, You know and see my struggles with self-discipline. I have a long "to-do" list, but I'm not on it. I don't take time to care for my own needs or practice needed disciplines. I feel like a failure in this area of my faith. It's easier to set rules for others than for myself. Help me become more disciplined when it comes to my health and the spiritual habits of studying Your Word and prayer. Amen.

O Lord, help me choose each day to do the right thing. That's a discipline that will keep me at the center of Your will. Amen.

Lord, this diet I'm on isn't working. That's probably because I keep pushing the boundaries and making excuses. I know I need to stick with this plan before my weight causes other physical issues. If there is such a thing as "God-enforced self-discipline," I need it. Strengthen my resolve, I pray. Amen.

Father, teach me to discipline myself—to see what I need to do and actually *do* it. Teach me to work hard even when no one is watching. Teach me to be trustworthy and dependable in all realms of my life. I am certain my life will be stronger, more stable, and more enjoyable. Amen.

SELF-ESTEEM/SELF-WORTH

The LORD values those who fear Him,
those who put their hope in His faithful love.
PSALM 147:11 HCSB

Precious Lord, advertisements and magazines are
brimming over with images of what is considered
beautiful, fit, and successful. If I look at them, I can easily
fall into the trap of comparison. Help me remember
that I am uniquely and wonderfully created by You, the
Master Designer. I'm a designer original and my self-
worth and esteem come from knowing how much I'm
worth to You. Amen.

Father, I've always been too sure of myself, too certain
of my personal worth. Remind me daily that my value
depends on who I am in relationship to You rather than
who I *think* I am. Amen.

Heavenly Father, I once considered myself to be worth
nothing. But now, I've discovered that I'm the beloved
child of Almighty God. Halleluiah! Amen.

Father, You call me Your daughter, Your child, Your
beloved, but I often forget who I am. I feel broken,
useless, ugly, and inadequate. Help me see myself as You
do—as the apple of Your eye—precious and cherished.
Empower me with courage and hope. Like a father
gently lifts his child's chin with his strong hand and
raises her face to look up into his eyes, so encourage me
today. Amen.

SERVANTHOOD

"If anyone serves Me, he must follow Me.
Where I am, there My servant also will be."
JOHN 12:26 HCSB

Dear God, give me a bigger heart to serve in more ways.
I ask for creative ideas and the ability to inspire others to
join in. Thank You for entrusting me with the honor of
being Your hands extended. Show me what is needed and
how to be a blessing each day of my life. Amen.

Lord, let me serve You. Give me a place to stand—no,
a place to kneel with an offering of service. Maybe I
can serve food to someone who is hungry or pass along
a warm coat to someone who is suffering in the cold.
Maybe I can encourage someone who is sick or lend a
helping hand to someone overwhelmed by responsibility.
I'm glad to give of my money and my time, Lord. I just
want to be a servant to others like You were. Amen.

O Lord, it would seem that I think too highly of myself.
I've overrated my own importance to Your work. The
other morning I woke up with a bad cold. I thought
about staying home but couldn't imagine how the
Kingdom could manage without my help. Oh my! Your
work depends on You, the Master, not on me, the servant.
Forgive me, Lord, and help me march back to my place,
trusting that You will let me know when I'm needed.
Amen.

SINCERITY

Let us feast instead upon the pure bread
of honor and sincerity and truth.
1 Corinthians 5:8 tlb

Dear Lord, sincerity is one of the things that matters most to me when interacting with others. Whether in business matters, friendships, dealings with the medical profession, or in spiritual circles, sincerity makes all the difference. Half-hearted or complacent attitudes, or simply going through the motions of caring, is not only meaningless but often harmful. Help me give my best in relationships and remember that sincerity is the evidence of my character, my care, and my witness. Amen.

Holy Father, when I say "I love You," I mean it with all my heart. Amen.

Lord, I want to think of myself as authentic—real, straightforward. Help me rid myself of pretense and hypocrisy. Help me nurture sincerity in every part of my life. Most of all, help me be the same person when I am alone as I am with others. I desire to live my faith out in honesty and truth. Amen.

Father God, once again I've had to deal with someone who backed out of a commitment with little or no explanation. It's hard to believe how insincere people can be these days. They seem to make promises and unmake them just as quickly. Rather than getting angry, Lord, I ask that You use this situation to remind me how important it is to say what you mean and do what you say you will do. Amen.

SINGLENESS

One who is unmarried is concerned about the
things of the Lord, how he may please the Lord.
1 Corinthians 7:32 nasb

Dear Jesus, I meet so many who struggle with being single. You are our greatest companion, and yet, we all have a need for human fellowship. Help me understand the challenges of being single so I can better encourage and help those singles I encounter. Give them a greater sense of Your presence so they know they are never truly alone. Amen.

Lord, You said Yourself that it is not good for human beings to be alone. I am alone, and I hurt. I feel almost desperate at times to find someone to share my life with. I ask You to send someone I can trust and develop a friendship with. Maybe You intend for me to stay single. Whatever Your intention, calm my soul into contentment at this stage of my life. Amen.

Dear Lord, I do feel the lack of a spouse at times, but more often I cherish Your interaction in my life. I know You've given me the gift of singleness so I can continue to serve You with all my heart and all my time. Father, I may never marry—or maybe I will. For now, I don't want to be chasing after what I don't have and forgetting about what I do have. I want to truly realize that You are all I need. Amen.

SURRENDER

*Give yourselves to God, as those who have been
brought from death to life, and surrender your
whole being to him to be used for righteous purposes.*
ROMANS 3:13 GNT

Dear God, I once thought surrendering to You was a
frightening thing to do. As I've walked with You and
finally surrendered all to You, I've seen that it's the
most freeing, trusting, and assuring thing I've ever
done. Thank You for giving me a surrendered heart to
love You deeper and more completely than I could have
ever imagined. Amen.

Father, my heart is a roamer; often I stray from the
sanctuary of my soul—from my God who loves me
dearly. I strive to follow my dreams and do my own
thing, yet I know that You love me and Your plans for me
are good and wonderful. I lay my life down, Lord, and
I trust You as You take it up and direct me anew. I want
Your plans, Lord. Amen.

Lord, Mom says surrender means to give up something. I want to give everything I have to You. Amen.

Father, when I'm struggling to surrender to Your will and
purpose, help me remember that You surrendered Your
life for me. That's the only reason I have an opportunity
to give my whole self to You. That sure does take the
sting out of it. I love You. Amen.

STRENGTH

He gives strength to the weary and
increases the power of the weak.
ISAIAH 40:29 NIV

Dear Jesus, Your Word tells me that when I am at my weakest, Your strength is perfected in me. I want to walk in that truth, Jesus. I have to remind myself that I don't always have to be strong; and there is a difference in being a strong person and someone who finds her strength in You. Thank You, Jesus, for being my shield, my protector, and my strength. Amen.

Lord, before me a mountain looms mysterious and overwhelming. How will I make it? How will I get beyond it? Is my journey over? Can't you move it? No? Then give me strength, power, and fortitude as I climb it! In the physical, I have little strength, but with You I can overcome. Amen.

Father, my physical strength is long gone. I've arrived at an age when I must depend on others to lift me up and take me where I need to go. Any yet, Lord, I know I am strong and vital in my spirit and soul. I know I can conquer all I come against in spiritual battle. I know I am a strong counselor to those who come to me for godly wisdom and counsel. I know I can assist others along the path to salvation. I am strong in You, Lord. Amen.

SUCCESS

He holds success in store for the upright,
he is a shield to those whose walk is blameless.
PROVERBS 2:7 NIV

Dear God, although tradition has taught me to wait on You for everything, Your Word also teaches that I have creative control over my life. You've blessed me with talents, ideas, and opportunities, but it's up to me to plant, water, and develop those gifts. Help me sow seeds of excellence and consistency as I act on and implement my goals for success in partnership with You. Amen.

Father, I want to be the successful woman You want me to be. Yet fear grips me and makes me unable to function. I know I should be brave and self-confident. You are my Father; what do I have to fear? Bless me with a dose of courage, and help me move forward and work toward my goals. Thank You for the good plans, the plans for success You have for me. Amen.

Lord, I see the looks some women give me. They feel I've never reached out for the success this world has to offer. But I know better. I have raised five wonderful children. In each I have implanted godly values and demonstrated before them the joy of having a relationship with You, their Creator and God. That's true success—success that lasts for eternity. Thank You for the honor and responsibility of being a mother! Amen.

TEMPTATION

*Blessed is anyone who endures temptation. Such a
one has stood the test and will receive the crown of
life that the Lord has promised to those who love him.*
JAMES 1:12 NRSV

Heavenly Father, there are so many voices clamoring for
my attention. The most subtle temptations sometimes
appear as opportunities. Give me discernment and
wisdom as I pray so that I will not act impulsively. Help
me remember that all that glitters is not God. Amen.

Father, I know there will be temptations, but I also know
You have promised a way of escape. Help me find faith
to withstand temptations. Build in me integrity that will
make me strong enough to flee sin. Give me strength to
resist the onslaught of the tempter. You said we "have not
yet resisted unto blood, striving against sin." It is true.
Help me, Father. Amen.

Lord, how do I know what temptation really is? Is it
anything that takes me away from You or anything that
doesn't please You? Amen.

I've been thinking about this, Lord. I would have fewer
temptations if I could only stay away from those places,
people, and things that promote the wrong thoughts,
words, and actions. Help me make good choices about
where I go, what I do, and who I do it with. Amen.

THOUGHTS

I will pour out my thoughts to you;
I will make my words known to you.
PROVERBS 1:23 NRSV

Dear God, so often my thoughts feel like a runaway train or an out-of-control wildfire. Remind me that when I take the time to surrender them to You, my thoughts will no longer control me. Keep my mind focused on and grounded in You. Let my daily thought-life reflect Your peace and grace to all those I meet. Amen.

Lord, I haven't been diligent in my efforts to keep my mind as pure as possible. I've allowed unsavory outside influences to enter in and put down roots. Sadly, I barely noticed their effect until You showed me. Detoxify and purify my thoughts, I pray. Help me turn away from defiling and harmful input and fill my mind with those things that are good and right, praiseworthy, honorable, and true. Amen.

Father, the Bible says that You think about us—we're in Your thoughts. I wonder how that can be. You are so strong and powerful and You have the whole universe to oversee. I pray that when You do think about me, You will smile. Amen.

I used to believe You weren't interested in knowing me personally. Thank You for changing my thinking and allowing me to experience the depths of Your up-close-and-personal love and compassion. Amen.

TOLERANCE

*We need to be sensitive to the fact that we're
not all at the same level of understanding.*
1 Corinthians 8:7 msg

Heavenly Father, the stresses of everyday life seem to
have dulled my sense of tolerance. My nerves are on
edge, and everything from loud noise to a sharp word
or rude behavior causes reactions I don't like. Being on
edge and impatient is not how I want to live. Help me be
more tolerant and more at ease within my own heart and
mind. Let peace settle in my soul. Amen.

Lord Jesus, You lived in a day of intolerance. You stood
against the religious who without thought or investigation
censured anyone who disagreed with them. Give me a
heart that can disagree with the belief of another without
disapproving of him or her as a person. Help me extend
grace to people who differ from me. Amen.

Lord, tolerance is a big word in our culture. We are to be
tolerant of every person, race, and nation. That I believe.
But we are also told to be tolerant of every word, behavior,
and action. Is that really what freedom is all about? Help
me understand when I should be tolerant and when I
should speak out. I don't want to be judgmental but I also
don't want to be tolerant of sin. Amen.

Heavenly Father, help me tolerate my brother. He's
always trying to make me mad. Amen.

TROUBLE

Dear friends, do not be surprised at the fiery ordeal that has come on you to test you, as though something strange were happening to you.
1 PETER 4:12 NIV

Dear God, I realize that no one in this life is exempt from trouble. My hope rests in Your promise to be with me when things go wrong. Be my way-maker, and rescue me when I feel like I'm sinking. Amen.

Father, when trouble comes, remind me that You are always there to stabilize and steady me. How awesome it is to know that You—the God of all creation—is able to carry me through any trials! When hard times come, You are there to reassure me. May I ever lean on You. Amen.

Father, trouble seems to follow my friend. Everyday there's some new disaster for her to deal with. I want to help, and I do reach out to her, but I'm beginning to wonder if there is more to the story. Are some people just unlucky? Is she doing something that makes her vulnerable? Can you help her, Lord? Take a look at my heart. Help me be the best friend ever. Amen.

Heavenly Father, I'm in big trouble. I did something I knew was wrong and now I've got to pay for it. Is there any way You can get me out of this jam? If not, will You help me get through it? Amen.

TRUST/DISTRUST

The Lord can be trusted to make you
strong and protect you from harm.
2 THESSALONIANS 3:3 CEV

Dear God, trusting You is easy in the light, when I see tangible answers. But trusting You in this dark place is not. Help me believe that You are working out all things in this situation for my good and for Your glory. Help me trust You with every detail, knowing my trust will be stronger when this trial is over. Amen.

Lord, I am in the habit of trusting family, friends, and even my own abilities before it occurs to me that I can trust You. Why am I so foolish? What brings me to such a place? You have the answers I need and the hope I crave. Teach me, Lord, to place my trust in You alone. Amen.

Father God, my parents warned me never to trust anyone. I've followed that advice. However, I find my lack of trust has left me feeling lonely and isolated. I don't like to live this way, but I don't know how to change. Show me one person I can trust, Lord—just one person to start with. In faith, I'm going to trust You to show me how to trust others. Amen.

I trust You, Lord, to keep all Your promises. I trust that You will continue to love me, feed me from Your Word, and show me the way through this life. Amen.

"If you live squinty-eyed in greed and distrust, your body is a dank cellar. Keep your eyes open, your lamp burning, so you don't get musty and murky."
LUKE 11:35–36 MSG

Heavenly Father, everything inside me wants to trust people, but disappointments through the years have caused me to become wary of motives. I've become pretty jaded. Teach me to trust again, but with discernment and wisdom. Help me open my heart to real trust, knowing that everything filtered through my solid trust in You will protect me. Amen.

Dear God, I'm praying for a couple who need a fresh revelation of Your love for them individually and together. They have lost their trust in You and in each other. Renew their love for each other and help them as they look to You to restore what has been lost. Amen.

Lord, some days I can't trust anyone—even myself. I worry and fret at night, rehearsing problems over and over in my mind. Help me trust You, Lord. Friends will fail me. Family members and my spouse will fail me. In the end, I will even fail myself, but my trust in You is always well placed. Amen.

Lord, what do you do when you can't trust the most important person in your life? What do you do when that person has told you lies? Show me what to do, Lord. You are the only one I trust. Amen.

TRUTH

*You are saved by the Spirit that makes
you holy and by your faith in the truth.*
2 THESSALONIANS 2:13 NCV

Precious Lord, make me a seeker of Your truth. Let Your Word saturate the very core of my heart and help me walk and live each day by the guiding light of Your truth. Amen.

My friend wants to know if I love her the most, Lord. How am I supposed to tell the truth without hurting her feelings? I know You'll give me the answer. Amen.

Father, I say I want truth, but often I would prefer a better story. I want to think I don't make messes and mistakes, that I am most often right, and that I always do my best. But I need the truth. Make me strong enough to hear it and grow in it. Let it be the agent of change I need so badly. Amen.

The truth is very difficult to find these days, Lord. We used to be able to trust what we saw and heard, but technology has blurred every boundary. I am going to pray before I move forward on anything, Lord. I will wait to see what You think. Thank You for being a beacon of truth, like a lighthouse on the shore, helping me anchor safely in the harbor rather than going aground on the rocks. Amen.

UNDERSTANDING

We ask God to fill you with the knowledge of his will,
with all the wisdom and understanding that his Spirit gives.
COLOSSIANS 1:9 GNT

Dear Lord, I wonder why we have to endure so much pain and heartache in this life and why our world is in such a mess. When things happen to me that are beyond my comprehension, help me turn every question over to You. You are the giver of peace that surpasses my understanding. Help me remember that there is a greater power at work than what I can see. Yours, Lord. Amen.

Lord Jesus, raising children is difficult. At times it seems impossible to deal with young people correctly. Often, I second-guess my decisions. I need wisdom, Lord, and understanding. I want to understand their issues, needs, and dreams. I want to understand their words and actions for what they are instead of how I take them. Make me a wise parent and one who never hears the words, "You just don't understand me." Amen.

I admit, Lord, I don't understand why You love me. After all, You're almighty God and I'm just a puny person. Besides that, I have so many faults that I can't even count them. Maybe I don't have to understand. Maybe I should just say "thank You" for this particular miracle and let it go at that. Thank You, Lord. Amen.

This much I understand, Lord. I'm blessed because You're in my life. Amen.

UNITY

He Himself is our peace and our bond of unity.
EPHESIANS 2:14 AMP

Dear Jesus, there is so much division in this world—
we see it in relationships, families, our churches. Jesus,
bring us together with Your purpose. Unite and ignite us
toward love and peace with each other. Amen.

Father, do we have to agree on everything before we can
be in unity? If so, I don't see how we can ever reach that
goal. Amen.

Lord God, our nation is split right down the middle.
Even members of the same family don't see eye to eye.
We've forgotten how to listen, how to reason, and how
to compromise. All we seem to know is how to lash out
with angry words and actions. I pray that as a nation,
we can put aside our selfish anger and get down to the
business of building a nation that is a blessing to its
citizens, its neighbors, and the world at large. Amen.

Father, help us as God followers to lay aside our petty
differences and come to You unified by our individual
stories of redemption. Give us love for each other and
strength to forbear and forgive. Teach us to pray for
one another and come to love each other in word and
deed. Amen.

VIOLENCE/ABUSE

He will redeem their life from oppression and fraud and violence,
and their blood will be precious in His sight.
PSALM 72:14 AMP

Dear God, how we need You to intervene in the violence
that is so rampant in this world. I can barely stand to
listen to the news or read the newspapers that tell daily
of more violence in the hearts and actions of people. I am
only one person, but help me make a difference through
my prayers, my stand, and my actions. Amen.

Father, protect us from the violence we hear about in
the news—war, crime, and unrest. Take care of us and
keep our families safe. Give us courage to face days and
situations in which we can serve You. Make our faith
stronger so that we are not hiding away. Violence has
touched us all and it is fearful, but take that fear from us,
God, and replace it with faith. Amen.

Lord God, I ask for Your protection from hurtful, violent
words—words designed to cut deeply and do great harm.
My mother used to tell me to shake it off, that words can
never hurt me, but words do hurt, especially words that
come from someone who professes to love me. I need
to learn how to protect myself from these onslaughts. I
need tolerance to remember there may be extenuating
circumstances like illness and pain. I just know I need to
find safety. Help me, Father. Amen.

He has not despised or scorned the suffering of the
afflicted one; he has not hidden his face from
him but has listened to his cry for help.
PSALM 22:24 NIV

Dear Father, my heart is breaking and I don't know
where to turn. Someone I thought I could trust, someone
I love, has been hurting me. I ask for strength and
courage as I take the first tenuous steps toward safety.
Help me as I seek a place to rest and heal. I ask You to be
close by my side as I go forward. Amen.

Heavenly Father, those who love me have suffered at
my hands. This fills me with guilt and regret. I ask Your
forgiveness for what I've done, and I pray for those I've
harmed. I know I can't overcome my abusive impulses on
my own. Guide me as I seek help in my struggle. Amen.

Heavenly Father, please help the hurting to stop. Help
my mom and dad love each other again. Until then, keep
us all safe. Amen.

Dear Lord, I pray for those who are the victims of abuse
around the world. I ask You to bring down those whose
greed allows them to traffic in human lives and those
who are on assignment from the Evil One to kill and
persecute Christians. I pray for those who are being
abused in their own homes. For all these and many more,
I pray that you would provide a way of escape. Amen.

WAITING ON THE LORD

With all my heart, I am waiting, Lord,
for you! I trust your promises.
PSALM 130:5 CEV

Heavenly Father, as I think about the tulip bulbs beneath a cold winter's ground, waiting for spring to rise up and bloom, I realize so much is hidden during times of waiting. I can't imagine Your purpose in my waiting, but I know that timing is everything in Your plan for me. Give me patience in Your waiting room, knowing that, even there, You are unfolding Your perfect design for my life. Amen.

Father, it seems You are an eleven fifty-five God. We ask You, and then we wait for Your answer. We need help, and yet we wait. We wait. We wait. You always come through for us; You provide for all our needs. But why is all the waiting necessary? Help me learn to wait in peace of spirit, knowing that You love me. Forgive me for my impatience. Amen.

My Sunday school teacher told us that after we finish our prayers, we are to "wait before You." I'm not quite sure why. Amen.

Lord God, it took me a long time to grow past my impatience and learn the wonder of just waiting in Your presence, basking in Your goodness, and soaking up Your peace and love. I'm so grateful that I have You in my life. Amen.

WAR

Scatter those nations that enjoy making war.
PSALM 68:30 CEV

Dear God, the very thought of war scares me. Living in a volatile world that changes daily, I struggle with not feeling secure. There will always be wars on this earth. I pray for those who risk their lives daily for the cause of freedom. Give those in the heat of battle the peace of knowing that, despite what we see or know, You hold this whole world in Your hands. Amen.

Lord, as my son goes to the battlefield, calm my anxious heart. Help me trust in Your sovereign will and know that whatever happens, You will give me the strength to endure it. I know that war is not Your plan, just one of the horrible results of man's sinfulness. I long for the day when men will destroy their weapons, and we will have true peace on earth. Amen.

Father, I pray for the victims of war around the world— families forced from their homes, children left orphaned, those who are injured and left to deal with the hopeless aftermath of violent conflict. These people's lives have been upended because of decisions made by their leaders rather than their own. I know You are there with each one. Thank You for caring so much, Lord. Amen.

God, can You hear me? We couldn't go to school because of the bombs and the soldiers. We really need Your help. We are afraid every day. Amen.

WEAKNESS

*My grace is sufficient for thee: for my
strength is made perfect in weakness.*
2 CORINTHIANS 12:9 KJV

Dear Lord, the little song "Jesus Loves Me" was one
I learned in Sunday school long ago. It reminds me
still today, that when I am weak, You are strong. Your
Word says that Your strength is actually perfected in
my weakness. Even when I feel the weakest, I have
confidence that You are holding me, Lord. Thank You for
letting me trust in Your might and strength. Amen.

Father, I know I have spiritual weaknesses. Guide and
bless me as I seek to overcome these weak spots. I have
physical weaknesses, too. As I age and when illnesses
develop, exercise and the right foods will help me regain
my health. Those spiritual weaknesses You long to rid
me of also need to be dealt with by exercising my faith,
praying, and feeding on the right spiritual food—the
truths from Your Word. Amen.

Lord God, no one wants to be weak—especially not me!
I've spent my life working to be strong, chasing down and
destroying weakness wherever I find it. And yet, I have
come to realize that my strength is fragile. It could be
taken from me in a matter of seconds. It's time for me to
acknowledge Your strength and my need, for the time is
coming when I won't be able to stand on my own. Amen.

WISDOM

*If you need wisdom, ask our generous God, and he
will give it to you. He will not rebuke you for asking.*
JAMES 1:5 NLT

Dear Jesus, the Galilean woman of the Bible wanted to
follow, serve, and know You personally. She wanted Your
guidance, wisdom, and Your presence. She was steadfast,
determined, and committed to understanding Your
nature. Jesus, give me a heart like the Galilean women.
Let me be a seeker of wisdom and one who applies it to
my daily life. Amen.

Lord, I need Your wisdom. Keep me studying and
reading Your Word, because I know that is the secret. I
know You will give wisdom to those who seek after it
with all their heart and soul. There is nothing that would
be of greater value to me and my family than the wisdom
that comes from above. I will search, Lord. Help me find
wisdom. Amen.

Lord, my father tells me that I'm smart but I'm not wise.
He says wisdom will come as I get older and learn more
about the world. I guess that means as I live through
different circumstances and gain experience. I do want
to be wise, Lord. I hope that I can be smart and wise as
well. I'm ready to start my wisdom training just as soon
as You're ready to start teaching me. Amen.

Father, show me who the wise people are in my life. I
want to spend time with them. Amen.

WITENESSING

"When the Holy Spirit comes to you, you will receive power.
You will be my witnesses—in Jerusalem, in all of Judea,
in Samaria, and in every part of the world."
ACTS 1:8 NCV

Dear Jesus, I've missed far too many opportunities to be a witness for You. I've passed people by that I knew needed to see Your love reflected in me. Forgive me for being slack and apathetic in this part of serving You. Help me shine for You and be a beacon of hope to those I encounter. Give me a greater boldness to share You and the Gospel everywhere I go. Amen.

Father, I want to share my faith in tangible ways with those who have not found You yet—who don't know the wonderful blessedness of being loved by You. Give me opportunities to tell others why I believe and how they can become Your sons and daughters. Lord, don't let me become merely a lot of noise and clanging, but with love, a true disciple maker. Add to Your family. Use my voice. Amen.

Lord God, remind me every day that my greatest witness is in my own home. If I can't persuade members of my own family that You are a good God who loves them, how can I possibly convince strangers? I know that it's more difficult to make my voice heard around those in my inner circle. They know me well—all my strengths as well as my weaknesses. There is no hiding my mistakes and frailties from them. Help me be a witness to my nearest and dearest. Amen.

WORD OF GOD

God's word is true, and everything he does is right.
PSALM 33:4 NCV

Dear God, I love Your Word. It's like a love letter and a
life-map, giving both direction and instruction. It's active
and life-giving when I pick it up and apply it to my daily
walk. Your spoken words never return void. Thank You
for Your Word. It is Your personal letter to all those who
are God-followers. Amen.

Father, today someone told me that the Bible is a love
letter from You to me. I promise to open it every day and
read what You've written to me. Amen.

Father God, I always find what I'm looking for in Your
Word. Each day I learn more about Your love, Your
justice, Your plan for mankind, Your sacrifice, Your
greatness, and so much more. Thank You for devising a
way for me to learn about You in Your own words. Amen.

Father, Your Word is a lamp that lights my path in the
darkness. Your Word has been a harbor in the storms of
my life. It has been a comfort in grief and a meal when
I am spiritually starving. It has been life-giving water
to my soul and strength when I am weak. It is health in
sickness, freedom when I am confined, joy in sorrow, and
a guide when I don't know which way to go. Amen.

WORRY

"Who of you by worrying can add a single hour to your life?"
LUKE 12:25 NIV

Precious Lord, You instruct in Your Word that I am
not to worry about any situation. Being human, I don't
always know how to lay my worries at Your feet and leave
them there. Help me completely let go of everything
that would keep me fearful and hinder me from trusting
You. Keep my heart set on Your power and grace,
remembering that it is alive and well and working on my
behalf. Amen.

Lord, if there is anything I am good at in life, it's
worrying. I seem to have trained myself in it. O Lord,
help me break free of worry and find an anchor for my
soul by trusting You. I see worry as the opposite of faith.
Change me and free me from the bondage of worry
through prayer and true faith in your caring love. Amen.

Father, I wish I knew how to stop worrying about
everything. I have a good life, a blessed life. And yet,
I worry that something will happen and I will lose all
that goodness and blessing. It must seem like a slap in
Your face, since You gave me everything I have in the
first place. I want to please You. I definitely don't want
to insult You. Open my heart to the truth that You both
give and sustain. What You have given, You are able to
protect. Amen.

WORSHIP

Worship the LORD with gladness;
come into his presence with singing.
PSALM 100:2 NRSV

Dear Jesus, there is nothing that quite compares to what happens when I begin to worship You. As I focus on You, my own worries and thoughts disappear in Your presence and Your peace. My oneness with You becomes joy and hope and grace all at once. When I set all else aside to worship and honor You, everything changes. . . in me. Thank You for loving me and meeting me in my moments of worship. Amen.

Lord, my voice may not be good enough to sing to You, but help me praise You anyway—worship You with my words and with deeds of kindness, with my hands and feet, with obedience and with honesty. Teach me to bow my heart and my head, to lay myself at Your feet and give You the worship You deserve. Amen.

Father, a friend asked me why I would serve a God who constantly commands me to worship Him. I didn't know how to answer her. But now I see this. You most certainly have all the worshippers You could want or need—the angels and all the other creatures of heaven and earth. I'm the one who needs to worship. It causes me to remember how glad I am to be Your child and how Your greatness makes my life so much more secure. That's for starters. Thanks, Lord. Amen.

MY PRAYERS

MY PRAYERS

....

....

....

....

....

....

....

....

....

....

....

....

....

....

....

....

....

....

....

MY PRAYERS

....

....

....

....

....

....

....

....

....

....

....

....

....

....

....

....

....

....

MY PRAYERS

MY PRAYERS

MY PRAYERS

....

....

....

....

....

....

....

....

....

....

....

....

....

....

....

....

....

....

....

MY PRAYERS

MY PRAYERS

....

....

....

....

....

....

....

....

....

....

....

....

....

....

....

....

....

....

MY PRAYERS

MY PRAYERS

....

....

....

....

....

....

....

....

....

....

....

....

....

....

....

....

....

....

MY PRAYERS

SPECIAL EDITIONS OF *THE BIBLE PROMISE BOOK*® FOR EVERYDAY ENCOURAGEMENT

The Bible Promise Book® for the Overwhelmed Heart

In *The Bible Promise Book® for the Overwhelmed Heart*, you'll find dozens of timely topics—including Comfort, Faith, Trust, God's Love, Grace, and dozens more—you'll encounter hundreds of verses from God's Word guaranteed to speak to your daily needs. This book is ideal for personal use and for ministries.
DiCarta / 978-1-63409-223-4 / $15.99

The Bible Promise Book® for Women

A beautiful gift edition for women features more than 60 relevant topics—including Adversity, Duty, Friendship, Modesty, Protection, Sincerity, Strength, and Zeal—you'll find nearly 1,000 total verses included. Each topic includes a brief introductory comment to put the verses into a 21st-century context. Handsomely designed and packaged, *The Bible Promise Book® for Women* makes an ideal gift for any occasion.
DiCarta / 978-1-61626-358-4 / $9.99